Tearing the Veil Hiding

God's **Only** Law

BILL COHEN

WestBow Press books may be ordered through booksellers or by contacting:

WestBow Press
A Division of Thomas Nelson & Zondervan
1663 Liberty Drive
Bloomington, IN 47403
www.westbowpress.com
844-714-3454

Scripture taken from the King James Version of the Bible.

ISBN: 978-1-6642-5577-7 (sc)
ISBN: 978-1-6642-5578-4 (e)

Library of Congress Control Number: 2022900996

Print information available on the last page.

WestBow Press rev. date: 2/11/2022

WESTBOW
PRESS®
A DIVISION OF THOMAS NELSON
& ZONDERVAN

CONTENTS

PREFACE

Why would I write a book about God's only law? Because my whole life has led me to it.

I had two significant influences, my dad and my grandmother, when I was young. And I lived in the space between them.

My dad joined the Merchant Marines during World War II. After the war, he was a professional boxer for a short time, and he taught me to fight for everything I wanted. He believed laws were suggestions to be navigated when they got in the way.

My grandmother escaped from Yugoslavia just before World War I. She was a Catholic and believed Jesus is the Son of God. She went to church every Sunday and lived her life following Jesus. She never preached Jesus. She just lived her belief. I felt her unconditional love and enjoyed countless hours learning from her, from cooking to just sitting down talking about life. I didn't understand the religion, the services were in Latin, and the memorized traditions were confusing; kneeling, standing, sitting, and reciting.

From the time I first remember going to church until I graduated from college, I was wild, and all of my learning about religion came from experiencing my grandmother's love. Once I graduated, my beliefs were tossed from wave to wave. They were continually influenced by the girl I was dating at the time or the friends I was hanging out with. Serious thought was not part of the process.

Then, one day I was 40 years old and had two young children. I was now responsible. What did it all mean? How was I going to teach them about life? What could I possibly bring to the table?

So, I began studying philosophers' beliefs, for they had devoted their lives to the subject. In chronological order, I systematically went through them from Socrates's logical arguments and his belief in a god, through Thomas Aquinas' first mover, and finally C.S. Lewis' attempt to validate his atheism, which led him to Jesus and the God of the Bible. Then, Lewis led me to read the Bible. So, I read the Bible daily, finishing it once a year for the next four years. Each time I read it, more layers of the truth became evident. Nothing else I had ever read was more truthful when viewed through the lens of real life.

In the past 30 years, many people have aided me in searching for the truth of this life. I am grateful for their caring and the love they have shown me. Some had provided insight when verses were confusing, some lived God's love as examples, and some challenged me when I was off the path to eternity. Here is a very partial list of those Godly souls: Mary Brajkovich, Billy Graham, George Vandeman, Dick Alesch, Steve Tiebout, Mark Finley, Shawn Boonstra, Mark Ferrell, Michael Youssef, Matt Chandler, and finally, the love of my life, Gail Cohen.

One of God's gifts to me is the ability to condense complicated information, leaving the essence to be absorbed without the distractions of unnecessary details. This is probably why I was drawn to a degree in Computer Science. This gift and the challenges the Bible presents are the reasons for this book. May you see the heart of the Lord in the pages you are about to read, and may His law of love draw you to Him, as it did me.

CHAPTER 1
A Kingdom Born of Love

God is creating His kingdom. The kingdom we first caught a glimpse of in the garden, the kingdom Jesus came to tell us about, the eternal kingdom of His love. His kingdom is being formed by volunteers who are choosing to be born again. When we are born, God breathes the breath of life into our bodies, "And the Lord God formed man of the dust of the ground, and breathed into his nostrils the breath of life; and man became a living soul." (Gen. 2:7). This first birth is of the flesh and was God's choice because He loves us and wants us to willingly choose to be part of His family.

So, He asks us to choose to be born again, "Jesus answered and said unto him, Verily, verily, I say unto thee, Except a man be born again, he cannot see the kingdom of God." (Jn. 3:3). This is our choice. However, only when we learn to love Him, as He loves us, will we be humble enough to accept His salvation and be born again of the Spirit; thus, following Him into eternity, "That which is born of the flesh is flesh; and that which is born of the Spirit is spirit." (Jn. 3:6). Jesus is trying to help Nicodemus, a ruler of the Pharisees, understand that entering the kingdom of God requires a rebirth of the Spirit, "Jesus answered, Verily, verily, I say unto thee, Except a man be born of water and of the Spirit, he cannot enter into the kingdom of God … Jesus answered and said unto him, Art thou a master of Israel, and knowest not these things?" (Jn. 3:5, 10). Jesus consistently taught the religious leaders they needed to reexamine their understanding of scripture. This rebirth takes us on the journey from living in the flesh to living by the Spirit, a process God calls sanctification, "But we are bound to give thanks alway to God for you, brethren beloved of the Lord, because God hath from the beginning chosen you to salvation through sanctification of the Spirit and belief of the truth:" (2 Thess. 2:13). God tells us that He created the sanctification process when He began creating. This process prepares us for life in His kingdom. God is watching us, and He smiles every time one of us chooses to go through the sanctification process.

"Beloved, let us love one another: for love is of God; and every one that loveth is born of God, and knoweth God." (1 Jn. 4:7). When we love God, we can decide to be reborn into His family by accepting Jesus as our Savior, "That if thou shalt confess with thy mouth the Lord Jesus, and shalt believe in thine heart that God hath raised him from the dead, thou shalt be saved." (Rom. 10:9). His law of love leads us to Christ's sacrifice, "But God commendeth his love toward us, in that, while we were yet sinners, Christ died for us." (Rom. 5:8), and to seek His righteousness and His kingdom, "But rather seek ye the kingdom of God; and all these things shall be added unto you. Fear not, little flock; for it is your Father's good pleasure to give you the kingdom." (Lk. 12:31-32). He then calls us to be salt, to flavor this world, "Ye are the salt of the earth: but if the salt have lost his savour, wherewith shall it be salted? it is thenceforth good for nothing, but to be cast out, and to be trodden under foot of men." (Matt. 5:13), and light, pushing back the darkness enough to lead others to Him, "Let your light so shine before men, that they may see your good works, and glorify your Father which is in heaven." (Matt. 5:16).

God created us, and He knows we are lost without Him, "The Lord is merciful and gracious, slow to anger, and plenteous in mercy … For he knoweth our frame; he remembereth that we are dust." (Ps. 103:8, 14). He knows He had to come to us, to draw us to Him, for we would not seek Him on our own, as the Israelites proved, over and over again, "And God spake all these words, saying, I am the LORD thy God, which have brought thee out of the land of Egypt, out of the house of bondage. Thou shalt have no other gods before me." (Ex. 20:1-3). We would instead create gods who would tell us what we want to hear, "For the time will come when they will not endure sound doctrine; but after their own lusts shall they heap to themselves teachers, having itching ears;" (2 Tim. 4:3), gods who would allow us to do as we please. We are just too selfish to have created the real God because we would not create a God who would ask us to be unselfish, "And the second is like unto it, Thou shalt love thy neighbour as thyself." (Matt. 22:39). Instead, we would create one we could use to control others, a harsh god who would punish people for their disobedience, the god the Pharisees brought us.

God hates to see us following false gods to our own death. So, He sent Jesus to show us how to deal with this world's sins and selfishness in the form of a man. While on the cross, Jesus completed the life the Father assigned Him, fully demonstrating He is willing to bear the pain and suffering of this life to save us, "When Jesus therefore had received the vinegar, he said, It is finished: and he bowed his head, and gave up the ghost." (Jn. 19:30). God's plan provides a way for us to escape to eternity. To access His plan, we must believe in Jesus and accept that we need to be patient enough to allow God's timing to work out. We cannot walk away from Him every time something bad happens. Despite the lies of this world, our sleepless nights, or the pains and sorrows of this life, we must remain faithful. For He has a purpose for each of us, who are willing to fulfill it.

Jesus's death on the cross introduced His new world order, one where those who had been unwelcome are now welcome, a world without force, where reigning means serving and everyone is loved, "But it shall not be so among you: but whosoever will be great among you, let him be your minister; And whosoever will be chief among you, let him be your servant: Even as the Son of man came not to be ministered unto, but to minister, and to give his life a ransom for many." (Matt. 20:26-28). Jesus came as a humble servant who was willing to die for us. When we look around at those who want to be chief among us, are they truly living their lives as unselfish servants?

Rebellion comes from our denial of God's love. We can witness this today in every part of our world, "Behold, what manner of love the Father hath bestowed upon us, that we should be called the sons of God: therefore the world knoweth us not, because it knew him not." (1 Jn. 3:1). Jesus exposed the scribes and Pharisees, "Woe unto you, scribes and Pharisees, hypocrites! for ye make clean the outside of the cup and of the platter, but within they are full of extortion and excess." (Matt. 23:25), to help us understand, the laws and ordinances those religious leaders created were not from God but instead born of the flesh. Those religious leaders were no different than those of us who today choose to ignore God and create our own gods, serving them instead of the real God. Unfortunately, religious leaders continue to use their created laws and ordinances to appear holy instead of demonstrating God's law of love, "And I saw a new heaven and a new earth: for the first heaven and the first earth were passed away; and there was no more sea. And I John saw the holy city, new Jerusalem, coming down from God out of heaven, prepared as a bride adorned for her husband. And I heard a great voice out of heaven saying, Behold, the tabernacle of God is with men, and he will dwell with them, and they shall be his people, and God himself shall be with them, and be their God." (Rev. 21:1-3). This is an example of our hardening our hearts and becoming stumbling blocks along the path to His kingdom.

When a member of the Sadducees came to ask Jesus a question, Jesus denounced him for his lack of knowledge regarding the scriptures, "Jesus answered and said unto them, Ye do err, not knowing the scriptures, nor the power of God." (Matt. 22:29). Those religious leaders had memorized every word of the law they created, but they refused to understand the Spirit of God's law of love, which He explained to them in the beginning. This is why Jesus called the religious leaders of His day hypocrites and vipers, "But when he saw many of the Pharisees and Sadducees come to his baptism, he said unto them, O generation of vipers, who hath warned you to flee from the wrath to come?" (Matt. 3:7). This is why He told us the parable of the Pharisee praying next to a publican, "And he spake this parable unto certain which trusted in themselves that they were righteous, and despised others: Two men went up into the temple to pray; the one a Pharisee, and the other a publican. The Pharisee stood and prayed thus with himself, God, I thank thee, that I am not as other men are, extortioners, unjust, adulterers, or even as this publican. I fast twice in the week, I give tithes of all that I possess. And the publican, standing afar off, would not lift up so much as his eyes unto heaven, but smote upon his breast, saying, God be merciful to me a sinner. I tell you, this man went down to his house justified rather than the other: for every one that exalteth himself shall be abased; and he that humbleth himself shall be exalted." (Lk. 18:9-14). He knows we have to humble ourselves to find Him, and this is the very reason He told us to pray in secret, to prevent us from becoming Pharisee like, "But thou, when thou prayest, enter into thy closet, and when thou hast shut thy door, pray to thy Father which is in secret; and thy Father which seeth in secret shall reward thee openly." (Matt. 6:6), and this is why Jesus was born in a manger, demonstrating His humble nature. Jesus does not want us praying for an audience, but instead, we are to pray privately, as if we are talking with a beloved friend.

When Jesus taught us to pray, "After this manner therefore pray ye: Our Father which art in heaven, Hallowed be thy name. Thy kingdom come, Thy will be done in earth, as it is in heaven. Give us this day our daily bread. And forgive us our debts, as we forgive our debtors. And lead us not into temptation, but deliver us from evil: For thine is the kingdom, and the power, and the glory, for ever.

Amen." (Matt. 6:9-13), He did not say, My Father, He said "our Father." He wants us to talk directly to Him, and when we do, we willingly demonstrate our belief in Him and our love for Him. Nobody loves us like God does. He has seen all of our flaws and still sees each of us as His priceless children. And He already proved that on the cross.

When we pray, we cannot be afraid to tell God everything. He understands because He already knows everything we have done and everything we are going to say, "Be not ye therefore like unto them: for your Father knoweth what things ye have need of, before ye ask him." (Matt. 6:8), and "For there is not a word in my tongue, but, lo, O Lord, thou knowest it altogether." (Ps. 139:4), and "For the word of God is quick, and powerful, and sharper than any twoedged sword, piercing even to the dividing asunder of soul and spirit, and of the joints and marrow, and is a discerner of the thoughts and intents of the heart." (Heb. 4:12). Our prayers are not for God. He is already perfect. They are pathways that bring us closer to Him, a step in our sanctification process. Just as conversations with friends deepen our relationships, prayers deepen our relationship with God. God is already totally committed to us. We can learn from Paul, "According to my earnest expectation and my hope, that in nothing I shall be ashamed, but that with all boldness, as always, so now also Christ shall be magnified in my body, whether it be by life, or by death. For to me to live is Christ, and to die is gain." (Phil. 1:20-21), who was totally committed to Jesus.

When we come to God in prayer, it should not be structured, preplanned, or with the ulterior motive of seeming holy. We can talk with Him, as we do with our friend, "But when ye pray, use not vain repetitions, as the heathen do: for they think that they shall be heard for their much speaking." (Matt. 6:7). Can we imagine our friend coming to talk with us and saying the same thing every day? How boring that would be. God wants us to speak to Him as a friend because He values our friendship. When we do, we learn to trust Him as a friend, as David did, "Come and hear, all ye that fear God, and I will declare what he hath done for my soul. I cried unto him with my mouth, and he was extolled with my tongue. If I regard iniquity in my heart, the Lord will not hear me: But verily God hath heard me; he hath attended to the voice of my prayer. Blessed be God, which hath not turned away my prayer, nor his mercy from me." (Ps. 66:16-20), and "The law of the Lord is perfect, converting the soul: the testimony of the Lord is sure, making wise the simple … More to be desired are they than gold, yea, than much fine gold: sweeter also than honey and the honeycomb." (Ps. 19:7, 10).

Religious leaders, both in Jesus's day and today, can either lead us to surrender to God's love, or they can lead us away from His kingdom. He wants us to discern the difference, "But there were false prophets also among the people, even as there shall be false teachers among you, who privily shall bring in damnable heresies, even denying the Lord that bought them, and bring upon themselves swift destruction. And many shall follow their pernicious ways; by reason of whom the way of truth shall be evil spoken of. And through covetousness shall they with feigned words make merchandise of you: whose judgment now of a long time lingereth not, and their damnation slumbereth not." (2 Pet. 2:1-3). Because He wants us to abide in Him, we cannot allow feigned words from false prophets to make merchandise of us. And He has dire warnings for those false prophets, "Not every one that saith unto me, Lord, Lord, shall enter into the kingdom of heaven; but he that doeth the will of my Father which is in heaven. Many will say to me in that day, Lord, Lord, have we not prophesied in thy name? and in thy name have cast out devils? and in thy name done many wonderful works? And then will I profess unto them, I never knew you: depart from me, ye that work iniquity." (Matt. 7:21-23). Notice, He said, "Many will say to me" and "I never knew you." This world is working hard to make merchandise of as many of us as possible. Sometimes it is sex trafficking, sometimes it is to capture our vote, and sometimes to control our actions. But what they are really doing is pushing us away from God. Those who have hardened their hearts blame God, or His followers, for everything bad that happens, including what they do themselves. This is how they continue to push us away from God. They keep telling us God is harsh, or there is no God, rather than learning God is love, which would teach them how to love. No one standing before Him on Judgment Day will be ashamed of their belief in God.

God wants us to understand that when we follow His way, we can avoid the pain and sorrows caused by our own selfish choices, which are the fruit of ignoring His Word. Divorce is an example of our rebellion, and it is regrettable because many are hurt by it. I speak from experience here, as my family and I were hurt by my first marriage ending in divorce. We were two non-believers lost in a marriage. God teaches us about marriage to help us understand what He means when He says, "For thy Maker is thine husband; the Lord of hosts is his name; and thy Redeemer the Holy One of Israel; The God of the whole earth shall he be called." (Isa. 54:5). We can depend on Him because He will always love us and never divorce us, as long as we say "I do" at the altar.

From the beginning, God told us to treat marriage as a joining of flesh, "Therefore shall a man leave his father and his mother, and shall cleave unto his wife: and they shall be one flesh" (Gen. 2:24), one flesh that should not be separated, "And said, For this cause shall a man leave father and mother, and shall cleave to his wife: and they twain shall be one flesh? Wherefore they are no more twain, but one flesh. What therefore God hath joined together, let not man put asunder." (Matt. 19:5-6). He wants us to be one with Him, "That they all may be one; as thou, Father, art in me, and I in thee, that they also may be one in us: that the world may believe that thou hast sent me." (Jn. 17:21). We can think of the principle of burning the ships, for we should not look back when we decide to marry. Of course, this is easier when both spouses are believers, "Be ye not unequally yoked together with unbelievers: for what fellowship hath righteousness with unrighteousness? and what communion hath light with darkness?" (2 Cor. 6:14). The movie "The War Room" might help those feeling trapped in a marriage with a non-believer. This movie describes the path to recovery when a marriage is not working.

When we understand the principle of God's law of love, we learn to live together, and divorce is no longer needed. No longer needed because we no longer desire another flesh beyond the one created in our marriage and all of our actions totally demonstrate our love for our spouse, "Nevertheless let every one of you in particular so love his wife even as himself; and the wife see that she reverence her husband." (Eph. 5:33), as all of God's actions demonstrate His love for us. When we love our spouse, as God loves us, we show our love to our spouse, and they will return it, never needing to fear us or doubt our love, as we never need to fear God or doubt His love. Instead, this ever-growing mutual love drives the lies and jealousy from our lives, as each spouse's love feeds the fire in their spouse's heart, as it has for my wife and me for over 40 years. This love nurtured, and growing foreshadows the ever-increasing joy we will experience for eternity as we live immersed in God's love. God gently calls us with His loving kindness, "Come unto me, all ye that labour and are heavy laden, and I will give you rest." (Matt. 11:28). And our marriages should reflect His gentle calling. God offers all of us His eternal love and devotion because this is the kingdom He is creating.

CHAPTER 2
Loving Like God

Think of us as blocks of marble at our birth. As we grow, we grab hold of this life's temptations and sins, and they create barnacles on our block, until one day, the barnacles completely hide our block, and we cannot recognize the person we have become. When we accept Jesus as our Savior, we can look into our spiritual mirror and begin chipping away the barnacles. As we abide in His love, we begin to see all the barnacles and eventually remove them. And, when we do, as Michelangelo saw David in the block he was about to carve, we can see the image of Jesus in our block. Then, we can begin the final process of chipping away everything that is not part of His glory, "But we all, with open face beholding as in a glass the glory of the Lord, are changed into the same image from glory to glory, even as by the Spirit of the Lord." (2 Cor. 3:18). The Holy Ghost is aiding us in this renewing process by holding our spiritual mirror to gaze into, thus allowing us to witness our progress. This is God wooing us with His overwhelming, never-ending, uninhibited love; and helping us put on our new man, "And have put on the new man, which is renewed in knowledge after the image of him that created him:" (Col. 3:10). God never gives up on any of us, continually showing us His love, no matter what we have done. Because He wants us to know He loves all of His children.

This sanctification process takes us from living selfishly to becoming selfless, like Jesus. As we work our way through the process, people see less of us and more of Jesus in everything we do. Taking the sanctification process from the theoretical to the practical is a worthy exercise, so here is a personal example of how this process spreads through our lives to the most minor things we do.

Near our home, there is a T-intersection controlled by a traffic light. The T Street leads to a hospital, and only people coming from or going to the hospital use that street. The other street has only one lane in each direction; however, it changes into two lanes approximately 100 yards before and after the intersection. Not sure why it was designed this way, but this is the reality that produces this opportunity to see our own sanctification in action.

For many years I would move to the newly created right lane in hopes of passing a few cars after the light turned green. I never thought much about it. However, during my daily Bible study, I read a few verses that caused me to reason with this situation and my behavior. It then became apparent that my behavior was not selfless. So, I modified it, recognizing that the cars in front of me deserved to keep their place in line during the temporary change in the number of lanes.

For the next few months, I remained in the original lane and watched cars pass me on the right. Experiencing the change in my emotions and attitude was eye-opening. First, I was upset that they would take advantage of me and the other cars they passed. Then, I felt my own self-righteousness raise its ugly head. My response was to make merging back into the continuing lane a little uncomfortable when their lane ended. Thus, an opportunity was born to reason with this new behavior.

Staying in my lane and not passing other cars was a demonstration of my love for my neighbor, "And the second is like, namely this, Thou shalt love thy neighbour as thyself..." (Mk. 12:31a). However, I have since learned that allowing my neighbors to pass me without complaining or being upset provided me the opportunity to follow God's advice on not judging others, "Judge not, and ye shall not be judged: condemn not, and ye shall not be condemned: forgive, and ye shall be forgiven:" (Lk. 6:37), and when I graciously allowed them to merge back into the continuing lane without harassing them, I felt my forgiveness leading me further in my sanctification process, "Then said Jesus, Father, forgive them; for they know not what they do. And they parted his raiment, and cast lots." (Lk. 23:34). Eventually, I learned my neighbors, who chose to pass me on the right, "for they know not what they do," had not noticed me or the other cars. They were just doing what came naturally, as I had been doing for years. God asks us to remove our barnacles. However, He does not want us pointing our fingers at others who have not yet become aware of their barnacles. The only way to help them is to love them, as God has loved us.

These are the lessons Jesus teaches us so that we might have peace in this life, "Peace I leave with you, my peace I give unto you: not as the world giveth, give I unto you. Let not your heart be troubled, neither let it be afraid." (Jn. 14:27). The peace I now have going through that intersection is seeping into other parts of my life, another barnacle removed and a step forward in my sanctification process, and it just might shine His gracious light unto those still unaware. Nothing I have given up to follow Jesus is worth comparing to the peace and joy He has already brought me. This is how we live the fruit of the Spirit, "But the fruit of the Spirit is love, joy, peace, longsuffering, gentleness, goodness, faith, Meekness, temperance: against such there is no law." (Gal. 5:22-23), and continue the sanctification process, "Ponder the path of thy feet, and let all thy ways be established. Turn not to the right hand nor to the left: remove thy foot from evil." (Prov. 4:26-27).

Why do we ever choose this world's temporary pleasures over God's endless mercy and grace? God calls all of our striving foolishness because He is already offering us the perfect eternal future, "Rejoice, and be exceeding glad: for great is your reward in heaven: for so persecuted they the prophets which were before you." (Matt. 5:12). What could be better than heaven's reward? So, He asks us to honestly avoid evil and seek good, thus demonstrating His love to others, "Let love be without dissimulation. Abhor that which is evil; cleave to that which is good." (Rom. 12:9). We cannot be drawn into the lie that the end justifies the means. God wants us to obey His law of love all of the time. So, we cannot break it in an attempt to force others to obey it. Yet, this is precisely what the Pharisees believed, and it drove people away from God. God's law of love in action allowed the early church to grow from the 500 who witnessed Jesus' ascension to over one-third of the Roman Empire before Constantine became Emperor. People lived the law of love, and others were continually drawn to it. That church was not a building or an organization; it was more significant than religion. Jesus living within the believers' hearts and their individual responses to Him led them to share His love with everyone.

We demonstrate God's love to others when we are tenderhearted and forgiving, "And grieve not the holy Spirit of God, whereby ye are sealed unto the day of redemption. Let all bitterness, and wrath, and anger, and clamour, and evil speaking, be put away from you, with all malice: And be ye kind one to another, tenderhearted, forgiving one another, even as God for Christ's sake hath forgiven you." (Eph. 4:30-32), and when we accept Jesus as our Savior, we become part of one body and mind, His church, abiding in His love, "So we, being many, are one body in Christ, and every one members one of another." (Rom. 12:5), and "Fulfil ye my joy, that ye be likeminded, having the same love, being of one accord, of one mind." (Phil. 2:2). This is how we know everyone in heaven will be living the fruit of the Spirit, totally in love with God and each other, "Happy is the man that findeth wisdom, and the man that getteth understanding. For the merchandise of it is better than the merchandise of silver, and the gain thereof than fine gold. She is more precious than rubies: and all the things thou canst desire are not to be compared unto her." (Prov. 3:13-15).

God's love produces the mercy and grace He created to save us from our sins, which then leads us to His sanctification process, "For we ourselves also were sometimes foolish, disobedient, deceived, serving divers lusts and pleasures, living in malice and envy, hateful, and hating one another. But after that the kindness and love of God our Saviour toward man appeared, Not by works of righteousness which we have done, but according to his mercy he saved us, by the washing of regeneration, and renewing of the Holy Ghost; Which he shed on us abundantly through Jesus Christ our Saviour;" (Tit. 3:4-6). The sanctification process, which Jesus has created for us, leads us from our birth, past the trials of this life, and ultimately to His eternal love, "But we are bound to give thanks alway to God for you, brethren beloved of the Lord, because God hath from the beginning chosen you to salvation through sanctification of the Spirit and belief of the truth:" (2 Thess. 2:13).

If we truly love God, we must love everyone else, "If a man say, I love God, and hateth his brother, he is a liar: for he that loveth not his brother whom he hath seen, how can he love God whom he hath not seen?" (1 Jn. 4:20), and "He that saith he is in the light, and hateth his brother, is in darkness even until now." (1 Jn. 2:9). It is so easy to fall prey to this world's lie that it is acceptable to hate another person. However, God says we need to love everyone, even those we perceive as our enemies, "But I say unto you, Love your enemies, bless them that curse you, do good to them that hate you, and pray for them which despitefully use you, and persecute you;" (Matt. 5:44), because there is no reward for loving only those who love us, "For if ye love them which love you, what reward have ye? do not even the publicans the same?" (Matt. 5:46). Therefore, when we say or show we hate someone, we are really saying and showing we do not know God.

God asks us to love even those who curse us, abuse us, and hate us, "Ye have heard that it hath been said, An eye for an eye, and a tooth for a tooth: But I say unto you, That ye resist not evil: but whosoever shall smite thee on thy right cheek, turn to him the other also. And if any man will sue thee at the law, and take away thy coat, let him have thy cloak also. And whosoever shall compel thee to go a mile, go with him twain. Give to him that asketh thee, and from him that would borrow of thee turn not thou away. Ye have heard that it hath been said, Thou shalt love thy neighbour, and hate thine enemy. But I say unto you, Love your enemies, bless them that curse you, do good to them that hate you, and pray for them which despitefully use you, and persecute you;" (Matt. 5:38-44).

God asks us to do this, so the sinner can witness an example of God's love and be drawn to God's way of treating each other, "Having your conversation honest among the Gentiles: that, whereas they speak against you as evildoers, they may by your good works, which they shall behold, glorify God in the day of visitation." (1 Pet. 2:12), which is part of my own testimony, as I have learned returning evil for evil only escalates problems and adds to our unrest. We are either living His law of love or rebelling against it. The reward for showing love to others is the deepening of our relationship with God, "Recompense to no man evil for evil. Provide things honest in the sight of all men. If it be possible, as much as lieth in you, live peaceably with all men. Dearly beloved, avenge not yourselves, but rather give place unto wrath: for it is written, Vengeance is mine; I will repay, saith the Lord." (Rom. 12:17-19). Jesus wants us to not only live peaceably, but He also calls us to be peacemakers, "Blessed are the peacemakers: for they shall be called the children of God." (Matt. 5:9). He wants us to actively live His law of love.

"Then came Peter to him, and said, Lord, how oft shall my brother sin against me, and I forgive him? till seven times? Jesus saith unto him, I say not unto thee, Until seven times: but, Until seventy times seven." (Matt. 18:21-22). God asks us to love others to the point of unlimited forgiveness for their sins against us, "For if ye forgive men their trespasses, your heavenly Father will also forgive you: But if ye forgive not men their trespasses, neither will your Father forgive your trespasses." (Matt. 6:14-15). Can we say Jesus is our friend and not forgive others?

Eventually, we learn to love everyone, allowing the flames of selflessness to incinerate the conflicts that destroy relationships. This can only happen when we abide in Him, "Abide in me, and I in you. As the branch cannot bear fruit of itself, except it abide in the vine; no more can ye, except ye abide in me." (Jn. 15:4), and "And we have known and believed the love that God hath to us. God is love; and he that dwelleth in love dwelleth in God, and God in him." (1 Jn. 4:16). This is how His love is perfected in us, "No man hath seen God at any time. If we love one another, God dwelleth in us, and his love is perfected in us." (1 Jn. 4:12).

God asks us to love everyone and to willingly lay down our lives for them, as He did for us, "Hereby perceive we the love of God, because he laid down his life for us: and we ought to lay down our lives for the brethren." (1 Jn. 3:16), while we were all still in our sins, "Surely he hath borne our griefs, and carried our sorrows: yet we did esteem him stricken, smitten of God, and afflicted. But he was wounded for our transgressions, he was bruised for our iniquities: the chastisement of our peace was upon him; and with his stripes we are healed." (Isa. 53:4-5). Laying down our lives might mean dying as martyrs; however, it also might mean giving up part of our lives by serving once a week at our local food bank, visiting widows, hospitals, or prisons, "For I was an hungred, and ye gave me meat: I was thirsty, and ye gave me drink: I was a stranger, and ye took me in: Naked, and ye clothed me: I was sick, and ye visited me: I was in prison, and ye came unto me." (Matt. 25:35-36), because we are all the least of these, "And the King shall answer and say unto them, Verily I say unto you, Inasmuch as ye have done it unto one of the least of these my brethren, ye have done it unto me." (Matt. 25:40), sinners trying to find our way to Jesus, "If we say that we have no sin, we deceive ourselves, and the truth is not in us." (1 Jn. 1:8).

Jesus went to the cross for each of us; murderers, liars, and gossips. We all start this life fully in love with ourselves and separated from Him. However, His sacrifice allows us to clearly witness His selfless love. He did this, so each of us could realize we have sinned and have the opportunity to repent from our sins. This is why He asks us to draw other sinners to Him, "For so hath the Lord commanded us, saying, I have set thee to be a light of the Gentiles, that thou shouldest be for salvation unto the ends of the earth." (Acts 13:47). We cannot be satisfied with finding Jesus ourselves. We are then called to introduce Him to others to the uttermost part of the earth, "But ye shall receive power, after that the Holy Ghost is come upon you: and ye shall be witnesses unto me both in Jerusalem, and in all Judaea, and in Samaria, and unto the uttermost part of the earth." (Acts 1:8).

Before he received the lethal injection, Dustin Higgs's last seven words were, "I am ok. I am at peace." Dustin could utter these words because he had accepted Jesus as his Savior and had repented from his heinous crimes. Someone introduced Dustin to Jesus, another example of the work Jesus began on the cross. Jesus calls us to be part of His continuing work, part of the process of going after the one, "What man of you, having an hundred sheep, if he lose one of them, doth not leave the ninety and nine in the wilderness, and go after that which is lost, until he find it?" (Lk. 15:4). He sent someone for us. Do we not then owe it to our fellow sinners to go after as many of them as possible?

God loves everyone, "Then Peter opened his mouth, and said, Of a truth I perceive that God is no respecter of persons:" (Acts 10:34), He brings the sun and the rain on everyone, without discrimination, "That ye may be the children of your Father which is in heaven: for he maketh his sun to rise on the evil and on the good, and sendeth rain on the just and on the unjust." (Matt. 5:45). But, unfortunately, this world promotes the opposite philosophy by dividing us into small groups who selfishly oppose each other, which leads us away from God. When we love as God does, we love everyone all of the time. We do not oppose any group, but we live God's law of love and give everyone the same freedom to choose. He will not force us to love Him, so He warns us about the broad path, which is the way of this world, for it will lead to our destruction, "Enter ye in at the strait gate: for wide is the gate, and broad is the way, that leadeth to destruction, and many there be which go in thereat: Because strait is the gate, and narrow is the way, which leadeth unto life, and few there be that find it." (Matt. 7:13-14). Instead, He wants us to choose the strait gate, which leads us to the narrow path where we will find Him, His love, and eternity.

When we ask God how our broken hearts can be part of His plan, we are really asking God to favor us over others. He will not play favorites because He loves us all equally. We cannot think God loves us more because we are somehow more deserving, for we cannot earn our way into His family. His free gift of salvation is offered to everyone, and He is giving each of us the opportunity to accept His love.

God is not creating the pain and suffering of this world. The collective "we" are by denying His existence, living in conflict with His creation, and rebelling against His law of love. He is letting us exercise the free will He gave us, and choosing to blame God for what we do, or others have done in rebellion demonstrates our misunderstanding of free will. C.S. Lewis states it best, "If a thing is free to be good it is also free to be bad. And free will is what has made evil possible. Why, then, did God give them free will? Because free will, though it makes evil possible, it is also the only thing that makes possible any love or goodness or joy worth having." God wants everyone to reflect His love, which is exactly what everyone will be doing in heaven.

We can picture ourselves sitting by a loved one on their deathbed. We can feel the ache of our loss deep in our hearts. This is the picture of God's love that is burnt into my mind, the image of Him sitting by us as we refuse His offer of eternal life with Him. He sent Jesus to die for all of us, but He has to witness those who refuse to accept Jesus's sacrifice. Sadly, millions of His children needlessly choose death, "For the wages of sin is death; but the gift of God is eternal life through Jesus Christ our Lord." (Rom. 6:23). No matter what we have done in this life, His love for us never changes, "For I am persuaded, that neither death, nor life, nor angels, nor principalities, nor powers, nor things present, nor things to come, Nor height, nor depth, nor any other creature, shall be able to separate us from the love of God, which is in Christ Jesus our Lord." (Rom. 8:38-39). All we have to do is accept it.

CHAPTER 3
God's Law of Love

When I first picked up my cross and began following Jesus, I did not fully understand His message. The only thing I was sure of was that He knew the way, "Jesus saith unto him, I am the way, the truth, and the life: no man cometh unto the Father, but by me." (Jn. 14:6). I have since learned this world has woven a veil made up of selfishness and lies to hide God's only law. Those lying to us want us to believe there are so many laws created by God and man that we cannot possibly keep them all. The implication is it is okay to break some of them, even God's laws, since everyone lies, cheats, steals, envies, or worse, now and again. So today, we are tearing this veil of selfishness and lies to reveal the truth that God has only one law. Everything else attributed to God is either a clarification of this law or others lying to us to keep us from His truth because they have chosen to ignore God. And, some of these liars are actually trying to manipulate us with their lies.

God's only law is His law of love, "And now I beseech thee, lady, not as though I wrote a new commandment unto thee, but that which we had from the beginning, that we love one another." (2 Jn. 5:5). He said this is the commandment we have had from the beginning, and we do not need other laws if we would just live the fruit of the Spirit, "But the fruit of the Spirit is love, joy, peace, longsuffering, gentleness, goodness, faith, Meekness, temperance: against such there is no law." (Gal. 5:22–23). This is God describing what His law of love looks like. And He tells us, all the law and the prophets are fulfilled in one word, love, "For all the law is fulfilled in one word, even in this; Thou shalt love thy neighbour as thyself." (Gal. 5:14), and "Therefore all things whatsoever ye would that men should do to you, do ye even so to them: for this is the law and the prophets." (Matt. 7:12), and "Owe no man any thing, but to love one another: for he that loveth another hath fulfilled the law." (Rom. 13:8).

This world uses the word love to promote many agendas, but God's selfless law of love is not what they are talking about. This world's substitute version of love is nothing more than self-love disguised. Self-love is dark, devoid of God's law of love. Picture a dark room. When we bring a candle into this room, the darkness flees because the selfishness that created it is no longer able to hide from the light of His truth, "For every one that doeth evil hateth the light, neither cometh to the light, lest his deeds should be reproved. But he that doeth truth cometh to the light, that his deeds may be made manifest, that they are wrought in God." (Jn. 3:20-21). It is God's selfless love that unveils the truth. And, as light and darkness cannot occupy the same space, love and self-love cannot rule the same heart; we either love as God does, or self-love will continue to grow in our hearts. So, the person who helps another out of love is not concerned if it is witnessed. Their reward is the joy of truthfully reflecting God's love. This is God's love lighting another dark room. Self-love calls us to proclaim our charity to show the world how wonderful we are. However, that will be our only reward, "Therefore when thou doest thine alms, do not sound a trumpet before thee, as the hypocrites do in the synagogues and in the streets, that they may have glory of men. Verily I say unto you, They have their reward." (Matt. 6:1-4).

God calls His law of love the royal law, "If ye fulfil the royal law according to the scripture, Thou shalt love thy neighbour as thyself, ye do well." (Jam. 2:8). The royal law shows God's mercy and truth, "Let not mercy and truth forsake thee: bind them about thy neck; write them upon the table of thine heart: So shalt thou find favour and good understanding in the sight of God and man." (Prov. 3:3-4). It also shows His humility and justice, "He hath shewed thee, O man, what is good; and what doth the Lord require of thee, but to do justly, and to love mercy, and to walk humbly with thy God?" (Mic. 6:8). So we are not following His law of love unless we are consistently humble, unfailingly merciful, always truthful, and continually seeking justice for everyone.

God gave us Jesus as the cornerstone of our faith and His law of love as a plumb line that points us to Him and His righteousness, which sweeps away all lies, "Therefore thus saith the Lord God, Behold, I lay in Zion for a foundation a stone, a tried stone, a precious corner stone, a sure foundation: he that believeth shall not make haste. Judgment also will I lay to the line, and righteousness to the plummet: and the hail shall sweep away the refuge of lies, and the waters shall overflow the hiding place." (Isa. 28:16-17). A plumb line that helps us understand His Word, "We are of God: he that knoweth God heareth us; he that is not of God heareth not us. Hereby know we the spirit of truth, and the spirit of error. Beloved, let us love one another: for love is of God; and every one that loveth is born of God, and knoweth God." (1 Jn. 4:6-7).

God is love. Those who learn to love as God does will know God and will use His law of love as their only plumb line to confirm what is from Him. Anything that conflicts with God's law of love is not from God. And we will choose to use His law of love only if we are drawn to it, "And I, if I be lifted up from the earth, will draw all men unto me … But though he had done so many miracles before them, yet they believed not on him … Therefore they could not believe, because that Esaias said again, He hath blinded their eyes, and hardened their heart; that they should not see with their eyes, nor understand with their heart, and be converted, and I should heal them … Nevertheless among the chief rulers also many believed on him; but because of the Pharisees they did not confess him, lest they should be put out of the synagogue: For they loved the praise of men more than the praise of God. Jesus cried and said, He that believeth on me, believeth not on me, but on him that sent me. And he that seeth me seeth him that sent me." (Jn. 12:32, 37, 39-40, 42-45). So He tells us about His love and then shows it to us.

In the Lord's prayer, Jesus invites us to live this life as we will in heaven, "After this manner therefore pray ye: Our Father which art in heaven, Hallowed be thy name. Thy kingdom come, Thy will be done in earth, as it is in heaven." (Matt. 6:9-10). This means we will be entirely in love with Him and each other here on earth as we will be in heaven. Those who willingly follow Jesus in this life are helping Him gather His children. When someone returns our love, they demonstrate their desire to be part of His kingdom. Others will reject God's offer and therefore will also reject us and our love, "If the world hate you, ye know that it hated me before it hated you. If ye were of the world, the world would love his own: but because ye are not of the world, but I have chosen you out of the world, therefore the world hateth you." (Jn. 15:18-19).

Jesus brought us a vision of heaven, "And God shall wipe away all tears from their eyes; and there shall be no more death, neither sorrow, nor crying, neither shall there be any more pain: for the former things are passed away." (Rev. 21:4). He also brought the invitation to live there for eternity, "Verily, verily, I say unto you, He that heareth my word, and believeth on him that sent me, hath everlasting life, and shall not come into condemnation; but is passed from death unto life." (Jn. 5:24). However, He is allowing each of us to choose for ourselves. Do we feel worthy of being loved unconditionally? God showed us we are, "For God so loved the world, that He gave His only begotten Son, that whosoever believeth in Him should not perish, but have everlasting life." (Jn. 3:16). Could He love us more? "Greater love hath no man than this, that a man lay down his life for his friends." (Jn. 15:14). What more does He need to do to prove He loves us?

Jesus tells a religious leader he is close to the kingdom of God because he understands God's law of love, "And one of the scribes came, and having heard them reasoning together, and perceiving that he had answered them well, asked him, Which is the first commandment of all? And Jesus answered him, The first of all the commandments is, Hear, O Israel; The Lord our God is one Lord: And thou shalt love the Lord thy God with all thy heart, and with all thy soul, and with all thy mind, and with all thy strength: this is the first commandment. And the second is like, namely this, Thou shalt love thy neighbour as thyself. There is none other commandment greater than these. And the scribe said unto him, Well, Master, thou hast said the truth: for there is one God; and there is none other but he: And to love him with all the heart, and with all the understanding, and with all the soul, and with all the strength, and to love his neighbour as himself, is more than all whole burnt offerings and sacrifices. And when Jesus saw that he answered discreetly, he said unto him, Thou art not far from the kingdom of God. And no man after that durst ask him any question." (Mk. 12:28-34).

Many who count themselves wise consistently try to ignore, hide, or mischaracterize God's law of love, leading others to disbelief. God allows this, "For it is written, I will destroy the wisdom of the wise, and will bring to nothing the understanding of the prudent." (1 Cor. 1:19) because He knows the wisdom of the wise is nothing more than some of us using our free will to rebel against His law of love. This happens when we look inward for wisdom instead of listening to God, "Let no man deceive himself. If any man among you seemeth to be wise in this world, let him become a fool, that he may be wise." (1 Cor. 3:18). Sadly, when we reject the wisdom God offers to all, we are left worshipping the creature more than the Creator, "Professing themselves to be wise, they became fools, And changed the glory of the uncorruptible God into an image made like to corruptible man, and to birds, and fourfooted beasts, and creeping things. Wherefore God also gave them up to uncleanness through the lusts of their own hearts, to dishonour their own bodies between themselves: Who changed the truth of God into a lie, and worshipped and served the creature more than the Creator, who is blessed for ever. Amen." (Rom. 1:22-25). When we think we are too smart to fall for God's simple law of love, we make up our own laws and set up our own images to worship, thus choosing to reject God and the eternity He is offering.

We worship money to create the temporary illusion of extreme wealth; attention-seeking because we feel insecure; power to elevate our importance; fame to draw others to worship us; biblical prowess to exaggerate our holiness. We use false science to legitimize our rebellion or appear intellectual;

pleasure-seeking to escape our lack of self-worth; and hatred because we do not feel truly loved. These are not examples of love but self-love. Dickens taught us the value of feeling loved, as Scrooge learned to love after finally feeling loved. Are we now worshipping ourselves rather than our Creator? Can we not see that rejecting God's love creates a hole we must fill with something?

God wants us to lay up our treasures in heaven, not in this life, "Lay not up for yourselves treasures upon earth, where moth and rust doth corrupt, and where thieves break through and steal: But lay up for yourselves treasures in heaven, where neither moth nor rust doth corrupt, and where thieves do not break through nor steal: For where your treasure is, there will your heart be also." (Matt. 6:19-21). He warns us about the moths, rust, and thieves because He wants us to understand everything is in the process of decaying and on its way to the grave. Nothing in this life is permanent. To prove this, we just need to stop feeding our rebellion long enough to see it decay. A garden left unattended is overrun with weeds. So, likewise, a life unattended is overwhelmed by addictions.

We, humans, have continually ignored God's warnings and rebelled against His simple law of love by creating our own laws, "There is a way which seemeth right unto a man, but the end thereof are the ways of death." (Prov. 14:12). God wants us to put His law of love before all the laws we have created, "Then Peter and the other apostles answered and said, We ought to obey God rather than men." (Acts 5:29). Our laws reveal our rebellion against His plan because we would not need them if we lived His law of love.

Our ideas of love and good and evil change with every generation because we do not surrender to His Word. We think we can create something better than God can. However, God's thoughts on love and good and evil never change. He can fully explain His law of love in the Bible, knowing we can read His message some two thousand years later, and it will not have changed. Can we not see how our rebellion has changed everything He created "very good?" "And God saw everything that He had made, and, behold, it was very good. And the evening and the morning were the sixth day." (Gen. 1:31). He designed everything to work together for good, "And we know that all things work together for good to them that love God, to them who are the called according to his purpose." (Rom. 8:28). And when we live our lives in alignment with His plan, we flourish and learn everything was created for Him, "For by him were all things created, that are in heaven, and that are in earth, visible and invisible, whether they be thrones, or dominions, or principalities, or powers: all things were created by him, and for him." (Col. 1:16). Yet rather than following His plan, we have turned wine into alcoholism, food into gluttony, work into pride, marriage into divorce, sex into perversions, exercise into obsessions, games into gambling and pride, and gatherings into divisions. God has called us to finish the race He has set before us, "Wherefore seeing we also are compassed about with so great a cloud of witnesses, let us lay aside every weight, and the sin which doth so easily beset us, and let us run with patience the race that is set before us." (Heb. 12:1). Instead, we willingly allow ourselves to become pawns in a rat race of confusion.

Would it not be better to seek the plan God has seen and work daily on the process of transforming our lives to align with His plan? "Trust in the Lord with all thine heart; and lean not unto thine own understanding. In all thy ways acknowledge him, and he shall direct thy paths." (Prov. 3:5-6). He continues to offer us His love despite our rebellion. We will not trust Him if we do not know Him, so we must first learn He is love, "He that loveth not knoweth not God; for God is love." (1 Jn. 4:8). Sure, He told us He is love, but more importantly, He showed us by dying on a cross for our salvation, "And walk in love, as Christ also hath loved us, and hath given himself for us an offering and a sacrifice to God for a sweetsmelling savour." (Eph 5:2).

Our pride is a self-defense mechanism we use to protect ourselves from the pains other people cause. We must lay down our pride before we can become vulnerable. "As long as you are proud, you cannot know God. A proud man is always looking down on things and people; and, of course, as long as you are looking down, you cannot see something that is above you." - C.S. Lewis. Only the vulnerable can become humble enough to reason with God's law of love. Humility tears the veil that has been hiding the truth, and it is our pride that created this veil, "The wicked, through the pride of his countenance, will not seek after God: God is not in all his thoughts." (Ps. 10:4), and "For whosoever exalteth himself shall be abased; and he that humbleth himself shall be exalted." (Lk. 14:11), and "Humble yourselves in the sight of the Lord, and he shall lift you up." (Jam. 4:10). We do not know everything, no matter how hard we pretend we do. So, there is no reason for us to become prideful.

Once we trust and obey God, His rewards can be clearly seen in this life, leading us to willingly and joyfully follow Him. He asks us to obey Him and experience what His plan will bring us, "Jesus answered and said unto him, If a man love me, he will keep my words: and my Father will love him, and we will come unto him, and make our abode with him. He that loveth me not keepeth not my sayings: and the word which ye hear is not mine, but the Father's which sent me. These things have I spoken unto you, being yet present with you. But the Comforter, which is the Holy Ghost, whom the Father will send in my name, he shall teach you all things, and bring all things to your remembrance, whatsoever I have said unto you. Peace I leave with you, my peace I give unto you: not as the world giveth, give I unto you. Let not your heart be troubled, neither let it be afraid." (Jn. 14:23-27). He wants to be our neighbor, "In my Father's house are many mansions: if it were not so, I would have told you. I go to prepare a place for you." (Jn. 14:2), and He wants us to love all of our neighbors, including Him, "For all the law is fulfilled in one word, even in this; Thou shalt love thy neighbour as thyself," (Gal. 5:14), which is why His law of love is all we need.

Once we obey God, we learn there are purposes and designs in everything He created. Then we can begin intentionally living in harmony with His creation, which leads us to His peace, "These things I have spoken unto you, that in me ye might have peace. In the world ye shall have tribulation: but be of good cheer; I have overcome the world." (Jn. 16:33), and "For God hath not given us the spirit of fear; but of power, and of love, and of a sound mind." (2 Tim. 1:7), and "For ye have not received the spirit of bondage again to fear; but ye have received the Spirit of adoption, whereby we cry, Abba, Father." (Rom. 8:15). Our ultimate reward is the expected end He is creating for us, "For I know the thoughts that I think toward you, saith the Lord, thoughts of peace, and not of evil, to give you an expected end." (Jer. 29:11).

Once we trust God enough to obey His Word, we gain His perfect peace, "Thou wilt keep him in perfect peace, whose mind is stayed on thee: because he trusteth in thee." (Isa. 26:3), and we learn the truth of His law of love. This experience propels our transformation, our sanctification and demonstrates it is the best way to live. We can never honestly judge His law of love if we have never experienced it, and we will never understand the expected end He is preparing until we do.

CHAPTER 4
Are We Sheep or Goats?

God's plan is brilliant. He gives each of us the freedom to choose our future. If we choose eternity with God, this life will be about introducing people to Jesus. Following Him brings us a life full of peace and joy despite the pain and suffering we will experience along the way. The pain and suffering of this world cannot be compared to the peace and joy that God's love offers, "For I reckon that the sufferings of this present time are not worthy to be compared with the glory which shall be revealed in us." (Rom. 8:18). If we deny Him and choose to live without His law of love as though we have only this life, that is what we will get, "And when thou prayest, thou shalt not be as the hypocrites are: for they love to pray standing in the synagogues and in the corners of the streets, that they may be seen of men. Verily I say unto you, They have their reward … For the Son of man shall come in the glory of his Father with his angels; and then he shall reward every man according to his works." (Matt. 6:5, 27). Notice He said, "They have their reward," and that reward will be this life only. The majority of the pain and suffering of this life is caused by people choosing to remain separated from God, and ironically, we create most of our own pain and suffering. No one lies to us more than we do, and no one's choices hurt us more than our own.

We need to stop blaming others for the problems we create. People are repulsed when we choose to be mean, affecting our relationships. Adultery is a choice, and it leads to divorce. When we choose thievery, it leads to prison. When we choose gluttony, it leads to discomfort. When we choose rebellion, it creates conflicts in our lives, and these conflicts cause the stress that leads to diseases, "A merry heart doeth good like a medicine: but a broken spirit drieth the bones." (Prov. 17:22). When we choose drunkenness, it leads to alcoholism. We could go on; however, God is giving each of us the choice to abide, "I am the vine, ye are the branches: He that abideth in me, and I in him, the same bringeth forth much fruit: for without me ye can do nothing." (Jn. 15:5). He thoroughly explains how our choices will affect our future in this life and for eternity. He wants us to focus on preparing for eternity rather than the grave by caring and sharing instead of being selfish. Yet, we keep choosing to rebel, and God responds by pursuing us with His eternal love even though He knows who among us will ultimately refuse His offer. He does this because He is love, and He loves every one of us.

God's plan includes Jesus coming to clarify the path to God, "Thy word is a lamp unto my feet, and a light unto my path." (Ps. 119:105). His Word lights the path to eternity if we choose to seek it, "Thou wilt shew me the path of life: in thy presence is fulness of joy; at thy right hand there are pleasures for evermore." (Ps. 16:11).

We all feel something inside, drawing us to eternity; this feeling lures us to fairy tales with happily-ever-after endings. Some try to satisfy this longing by finding substitutes in this world, such as temporary pleasures, fame, or fortune. But these attempts will never work, for they will end with this life. We just need to understand the one drawing us toward eternity is Jesus. He is calling us to our eternal home. Unfortunately, since He placed the desire for eternity in our hearts, when we sense eternity is beyond our grasp, it affects our mental health, and we are left feeling hopeless.

Religious leaders throughout history have whispered lies about God to lead us into slavery to their form of religion. Sometimes, they even attempt to add burdens, "The scribes and the Pharisees sit in Moses' seat … For they bind heavy burdens and grievous to be borne, and lay them on men's shoulders; but they themselves will not move them with one of their fingers." (Matt. 23:2, 4). But God's yoke is easy, and we can bear it, "Come unto me, all ye that labour and are heavy laden, and I will give you rest. Take my yoke upon you, and learn of me; for I am meek and lowly in heart: and ye shall find rest unto your souls. For my yoke is easy, and my burden is light." (Matt. 11:28–30). We are not to follow anyone but Jesus, "Is Christ divided? was Paul crucified for you? or were ye baptized in the name of Paul?" (1 Cor. 1:13), because Jesus is the only one leading us to eternity, "Neither is there salvation in any other: for there is none other name under heaven given among men, whereby we must be saved." (Acts 4:12).

When we see all of the laws, ordinances, and rituals religious leaders have created, we do not feel loved but instead feel we are under some impossible burden intended to show us how worthless we are, how hopeless our lives are, and how dependent we are on some form of atonement. Jesus came to prove His love is great, His burden is light, "For this is the love of God, that we keep his commandments: and his commandments are not grievous." (1 Jn. 5:3), His love is unconditional, "For I am persuaded, that neither death, nor life, nor angels, nor principalities, nor powers, nor things present, nor things to come, Nor height, nor depth, nor any other creature, shall be able to separate us from the love of God, which is in Christ Jesus our Lord." (Rom. 8:38-39). The path to salvation is our honest acceptance of Jesus's sacrifice on the cross, "I am crucified with Christ: nevertheless I live; yet not I, but Christ liveth in me: and the life which I now live in the flesh I live by the faith of the Son of God, who loved me, and gave himself for me." (Gal. 2:20), and Jesus's resurrection brings us His eternal hope, "Now the God of hope fill you with all joy and peace in believing, that ye may abound in hope, through the power of the Holy Ghost." (Rom. 15:13).

"Every word of God is pure: he is a shield unto them that put their trust in him. Add thou not unto his words, lest he reprove thee, and thou be found a liar." (Prov. 30:5-6). The Bible is the infallible Word of God leading us to Him, even when the devil tries to lead us astray. We can repel the devil by using God's Word, as Jesus demonstrated for us in the desert, "Then saith Jesus unto him, Get thee hence, Satan: for it is written, Thou shalt worship the Lord thy God, and him only shalt thou serve. Then the devil leaveth him, and, behold, angels came and ministered unto him." (Matt. 4:10-11). If we do not reason with God, we will not obtain the faith needed to understand His unchanging truth, that is older than time itself, which leads us to His promise, "But without faith it is impossible to please him: for he that cometh to God must believe that he is, and that he is a rewarder of them that diligently seek him." (Heb. 11:6), and we will not learn His love has never changed. Only our understanding of it changes as we allow His truth to remove the perceived conflicts we mistakenly see in His Word or to expose the lies this world propagates.

Why would some religious leaders add to, or change, God's Word? Because they have accepted fables created by prior religious leaders, or they have placed the approval of others, the desire for power, or personal comfort, above the Word of God. Many like their good life more than they want to save others, "Beware of the scribes, which desire to walk in long robes, and love greetings in the markets, and the highest seats in the synagogues, and the chief rooms at feasts; Which devour widows' houses, and for a shew make long prayers: the same shall receive greater damnation." (Lk. 20:46-47). However, God calls us to be servants, "But he that is greatest among you shall be your servant." (Matt. 23:11), and Jesus demonstrated it, "After that he poureth water into a bason, and began to wash the disciples' feet, and to wipe them with the towel wherewith he was girded." (Jn. 13:6), and we will all reap what we sow, "Be not deceived; God is not mocked: for whatsoever a man soweth, that shall he also reap." (Gal. 6:7).

"Suppose ye that I am come to give peace on earth? I tell you, Nay; but rather division:" (Lk. 12:51), Jesus did not come to give peace to everyone on earth, but rather, He came to show us the path to His kingdom. We are in the process of dividing ourselves into two groups, those who are with Him and those who are against Him, "He that is not with me is against me; and he that gathereth not with me scattereth abroad." (Matt. 12:30). We are either part of the solution or part of the problem. He asks us to be part of the solution, which means we love everyone all of the time. He has named these two groups, the sheep and the goats, "And before him shall be gathered all nations: and he shall separate them one from another, as a shepherd divideth his sheep from the goats:" (Matt. 25:32). In this life, we will choose which group we want to be in. We cannot allow ourselves to be fooled into believing there are other groups. We are either gathering with Jesus, or we are goats.

Those of us choosing to be sheep willingly follow Jesus into His kingdom. Those of us who want to be our own god, attempting to create our own version of eternity, our own kingdom, will gladly take the goat's name (Greatest of All Time) because we believe, as Lucifer did, this is who we have become. Others will not want to decide and will not reason with God. Our refusal to choose will leave us with the default decision of being a goat. God has made it very clear; we have to make a decision to receive salvation, "I call heaven and earth to record this day against you, that I have set before you life and death, blessing and cursing: therefore choose life, that both thou and thy seed may live:" (Deut. 30:19), so, we are either choosing to be on God's side, or we will have chosen to be against Him. There are no other choices. And, God will eventually separate these groups, "And he shall set the sheep on his right hand, but the goats on the left. Then shall the King say unto them on his right hand, Come, ye blessed of my Father, inherit the kingdom prepared for you from the foundation of the world:" (Matt. 25:33-34).

He asks us to open the door to our hearts and minds, "Behold, I stand at the door, and knock: if any man hear my voice, and open the door, I will come in to him, and will sup with him, and he with me." (Rev. 3.20), so we can reason with His truth and learn of His great love for us, which we experience fulfilled in His great joy, "And now come I to thee; and these things I speak in the world, that they might have my joy fulfilled in themselves." (Jn. 17:13), and only those of us who choose to be sheep will find His peace and joy, in this life and the next, "Now the God of hope fill you with all joy and peace in believing, that ye may abound in hope, through the power of the Holy Ghost." (Rom. 15:13). If we want to understand that circumstances do not dictate our peace and joy, we need only look to Paul and Silas in prison, "And at midnight Paul and Silas prayed, and sang praises unto God: and the prisoners heard them." (Jn. 16:25), as they rested in Jesus's peace and joy because they knew their treasure is in heaven.

My favorite pastor, Matt Chandler, has defined convergent space as a moment in time when heaven and earth kiss. This is the moment we feel heaven's presence here on earth. It is what allows us to live in Jesus' peace when the storms of this life surround us, "But when he saw the wind boisterous, he was afraid; and beginning to sink, he cried, saying, Lord, save me. And immediately Jesus stretched forth his hand, and caught him, and said unto him, O thou of little faith, wherefore didst thou doubt?" (Matt. 14:30). It helps us understand we have a choice; we are not imprisoned by the chaos of this world. This is Jesus extending His hand for us to grab hold of the peace He freely offers.

God wants us to be fully known by Him and by the rest of His family. This is what He taught us in the garden, "And they were both naked, the man and his wife, and were not ashamed." (Gen. 2:25). This message is not about nudity. He is talking about living openly honest lives filled with peace and joy. Understanding this frees us from the lies of this world. Unfortunately, Adam and Eve paid a high price to learn this lesson, which caused them to hide and mistakenly cover up their nudity, "And the Lord God called unto Adam, and said unto him, Where art thou? And he said, I heard thy voice in the garden, and I was afraid, because I was naked; and I hid myself." (Gen. 3:9-10). But it was not their nudity they needed to cover; it was their rebellion, and there is no way to hide it. Therefore, we need to stop trying to hide, give up our secrets, and become fully known by all. This is what confessing and repenting accomplish. Unfortunately, we are afraid to confess because we feel we do not deserve

27

forgiveness. The truth is none of us deserve it. That is the point; and why we need to confess and repent. This is part of the process of accepting God's free gift of salvation.

"For now we see through a glass, darkly; but then face to face: now I know in part; but then shall I know even as also I am known." (1 Cor. 13:12). In heaven, we will all be fully known, with nothing to hide, no guilt, no shame, only an atmosphere filled with love. We will no longer doubt God, as some of the eleven did just before He gave them the great commission, "Then the eleven disciples went away into Galilee, into a mountain where Jesus had appointed them. And when they saw him, they worshipped him: but some doubted." (Matt. 28:16-17), or, blame others, as Adam did in the garden, "And the man said, The woman whom thou gavest to be with me, she gave me of the tree, and I did eat." (Gen. 3:12). In this dying world, the goats will be unable to hear the voice of God over the noise of their guilt and shame. The goats will continue to hide their sins in the darkness, blaming others for their mistakes and pretending they are perfect. Pretending we are perfect leaves no room in our lives to find the door to eternity. We become too busy to reason with the truth. Only when we surrender all of our guilt and shame to His love will we be able to find our way to eternity. And, when we do surrender, everything changes. We become ever more peaceful and patient. We begin living lives centered on serving, and this world notices as we become God's shining lights.

If Jesus had not died on that cross to save us, our belief would be futile, His gift would not be real, and we would be the most miserable of all people, "For if the dead rise not, then is not Christ raised: And if Christ be not raised, your faith is vain; ye are yet in your sins. Then they also which are fallen asleep in Christ are perished. If in this life only we have hope in Christ, we are of all men most miserable." (1 Cor. 15:16-19), miserable because we will have given up some of the temporary pleasures of this life without the benefit of eternity. But Jesus has promised to return and take us to live with him for eternity, "In my Father's house are many mansions: if it were not so, I would have told you. I go to prepare a place for you. And if I go and prepare a place for you, I will come again, and receive you unto myself; that where I am, there ye may be also." (Jn. 14:2-3), and only our rebellion prevents us from believing it, "But he turned, and said unto Peter, Get thee behind me, Satan: thou art an offence unto me: for thou savourest not the things that be of God, but those that be of men." (Matt. 16:23). Peter is being rebuked so we can see how deadly our vain ambitions are and how poisonous our pride can be.

Rebelling against God's plan is the ultimate demonstration of futility. Nothing lasting or worthwhile is gained by it, and eternity is lost.

Jesus points us to the cross, so we might learn to follow Him into eternity as part of His family. He left a message for Peter, after His resurrection, "But go your way, tell his disciples and Peter that he goeth before you into Galilee: there shall ye see him, as he said unto you." (Mk. 16:7), so Peter would know Jesus forgave him and wanted him to be part of His eternal family.

Jesus wants all of us to know, His forgiveness has been offered to every one of us. This is why He left us so many witnesses to His majesty, "For we have not followed cunningly devised fables, when we made known unto you the power and coming of our Lord Jesus Christ, but were eyewitnesses of his majesty. For he received from God the Father honour and glory, when there came such a voice to him from the excellent glory, This is my beloved Son, in whom I am well pleased." (2 Pet. 2:16-17), and His resurrection, "Then the same day at evening, being the first day of the week, when the doors were shut where the disciples were assembled for fear of the Jews, came Jesus and stood in the midst, and saith unto them, Peace be unto you. And when he had so said, he shewed unto them his hands and his side. Then were the disciples glad, when they saw the Lord." (Jn. 20:19-20), and "Afterward he appeared unto the eleven as they sat at meat, and upbraided them with their unbelief and hardness of heart, because they believed not them which had seen him after he was risen. And he said unto them, Go ye into all the world, and preach the gospel to every creature." (Mk. 16:14-15), and His ascension, "And it came to pass, while he blessed them, he was parted from them, and carried up into heaven. And they worshipped him, and returned to Jerusalem with great joy:" (Lk. 24:51-52).

Love is essential to God, "Jesus answered and said unto him, If a man love me, he will keep my words: and my Father will love him, and we will come unto him, and make our abode with him." (Jn. 14:23). Can we not see Jesus wants us to choose to be part of His family? "For as many as are led by the Spirit of God, they are the sons of God." (Rom. 8:14). God invites us to become His sons and daughters; brothers and sisters of Jesus, "For ye have not received the spirit of bondage again to fear; but ye have received the Spirit of adoption, whereby we cry, Abba, Father." (Rom. 8:15), as His Spirit beareth witness, "The Spirit itself beareth witness with our spirit, that we are the children of God: And if children, then heirs; heirs of God, and joint-heirs with Christ; if so be that we suffer with him, that we may be also glorified together." (Rom. 8:16-17). And, so, He offers us this choice, "I call heaven and earth to record this day against you, that I have set before you life and death, blessing and cursing: therefore choose life, that both thou and thy seed may live:" (Deut. 30:19).

We need to choose to become sheep, willingly following our shepherd, Jesus. He promises us an eternity filled with love, where everyone will love everyone else. The kind of love Jesus leads us to is the only kind possible in the eternal family He is creating, for there will be no more pain, and no more tears, "And God shall wipe away all tears from their eyes; and there shall be no more death, neither sorrow, nor crying, neither shall there be any more pain: for the former things are passed away." (Rev. 21:4). And He is looking for volunteers.

CHAPTER 5
Our Pride or God's Selfless Love?

God's love is selfless, and those who love as God does will always put the happiness of others before their own happiness. Because God loves us, He wants us to experience His peace and joy, which exceeds our wildest idea of happiness. He knows nothing can make us more joyful than abiding in His love, "And it came to pass, while he blessed them, he was parted from them, and carried up into heaven. And they worshipped him, and returned to Jerusalem with great joy:" (Lk. 24:51-52), so, He draws us with His loving kindness, "The Lord hath appeared of old unto me, saying, Yea, I have loved thee with an everlasting love: therefore with lovingkindness have I drawn thee." (Jer. 31:3), and asks us to reflect His love to draw others to Him, "For so hath the Lord commanded us, saying, I have set thee to be a light of the Gentiles, that thou shouldest be for salvation unto the ends of the earth." (Lk. 8:16).

He has already demonstrated His desire to live with us, by walking with us in the garden, "And they heard the voice of the Lord God walking in the garden in the cool of the day:" (Gen. 3:8), again, when Jesus came Himself to live with us, "For whosoever shall do the will of my Father which is in heaven, the same is my brother, and sister, and mother." (Matt. 12:50), and He also promises us eternity with Him, "And I heard a great voice out of heaven saying, Behold, the tabernacle of God is with men, and he will dwell with them, and they shall be his people, and God himself shall be with them, and be their God." (Rev. 21:3).

Only the unselfish will be drawn to God and draw others to His light by reflecting it. It is our willingness to humble ourselves, which opens our hearts and draws us to Him, "No man can come to me, except the Father which hath sent me draw him: and I will raise him up at the last day." (Jn. 6:44). If we are selfish, our hearts harden, we disdain humility, and we will not surrender to God's law of love. Instead, we will think our way is better, "There is a way which seemeth right unto a man, but the end thereof are the ways of death." (Prov. 14:12). God does not force us to follow Him. He allows each of us to exercise the free will He has given us. He lets us live this life any way we want; still, He continues to offer us His love and eternity, until the day we die. Then, He will respect our ultimate decision, for we cannot expect Him to allow us to bring the chaos and cruelty of this world into the next.

God is pure love, "He that loveth not knoweth not God; for God is love." (1 Jn. 4:8). And He asks us to love as He does, "A new commandment I give unto you, That ye love one another; as I have loved you, that ye also love one another." (Jn. 13:34), which means we allow others the freedom to deny our love, as well as His. The unselfish do not try to control others, but instead, they enable others to fully live this life any way they choose, reflecting what God has done for each of us.

My personal feelings of fear caused me to withhold my forgiveness, disobeying God and thinking I would be somehow safer. However, I was missing out on this part of His plan. He wants to use us to draw others to His love. When people see us loving and forgiving everyone and contrast that with the evil those who refuse God's love do to us, they are drawn to God. This happened when the early Christian church flourished, despite being tortured and killed. This is what is currently happening in many countries, like Iran. Of the roughly 85M people living in Iran, about 1M now call themselves Christians. This underground church has no buildings. It is not an organized church, no denominations, just people meeting in people's homes and sharing His love. This is how the early Christian church grew, and this Iranian church is one of the fastest-growing Christian churches globally, despite the fact they need to hide to worship and are being persecuted and threatened with death. To better understand what is going on in Iran today, we can watch the movie "Sheep Among Wolves." When we finally accept God's perfect love, fear is cast out of our lives, and forgiving others becomes easy, for we can see past our present situation to the eternal future He has promised, "There is no fear in love; but perfect love casteth out fear: because fear hath torment. He that feareth is not made perfect in love." (1 Jn. 4:18).

This is His love in action, as He knows we are stronger when we surrender to His law of love, "And he said unto me, My grace is sufficient for thee: for my strength is made perfect in weakness. Most gladly therefore will I rather glory in my infirmities, that the power of Christ may rest upon me." (2 Cor. 12:9). When we pretend our strength is sufficient, we cannot be humble enough to allow His strength to be perfected in our weakness. This is one of the ways our pride keeps us from Him. The key is living within His plan for our lives, which He calls abiding in Him, "If ye abide in me, and my words abide in you, ye shall ask what ye will, and it shall be done unto you." (Jn. 15:7). When we abide in His love, we will not ask God for something that opposes His nature. Therefore, we will receive what we ask for in this life or the next. This is possible because we are no longer fighting against God's plan.

However, if we ask for something that does not fit into His plan, He will say no. We must accept that there will be things we want in this life, which we will not receive. Jesus illustrated this for us, including that we must always be willing to accept the Father's answer, "And he said, Abba, Father, all things are possible unto thee; take away this cup from me: nevertheless not what I will, but what thou wilt." (Mk. 14:36). Jesus showed He believes the Father has seen the future and knows what is best for us, "And we know that all things work together for good to them that love God, to them who are the called according to his purpose." (Rom. 8:28). The faith created by this attitude leads us to love as Jesus loves, "This is my commandment, That ye love one another, as I have loved you." (Jn. 15:12). He does not ask us to do what He is unwilling to do.

Jesus came to show us what God's love looks like and to deliver us from the fear and selfishness of this world. Once we understand this, we gain the faith that leads us to His will for us, "But let him ask in faith, nothing wavering. For he that wavereth is like a wave of the sea driven with the wind and tossed." (Jam. 1:6), and His will leads us to do our part in tending His garden, "And the Lord God took the man, and put him into the garden of Eden to dress it and to keep it." (Gen. 2:15). God created us to be part of the solution, not part of the problem. Doing our part means we tend the soil and plant the seeds, "And he spake many things unto them in parables, saying, Behold, a sower went forth to sow … But other fell into good ground, and brought forth fruit, some an hundredfold, some sixtyfold, some thirtyfold." (Matt. 13:3, 8). But, of course, not all of the seeds we sow fall on good ground, "When any one heareth the word of the kingdom, and understandeth it not, then cometh the wicked one, and catcheth away that which was sown in his heart. This is he which received seed by the way side." (Matt. 13:19). We are to keep sowing because even though not everyone who hears us will choose to be saved, it does help the soul who desires to hear the Word, witnesses His love in our behavior, and is then drawn to reason with God. We cannot say we are Christians if we refuse to align our behavior with His law of love, "And have no fellowship with the unfruitful works of darkness, but rather reprove them." (Eph. 5:11).

God tells us to allow the tares to grow alongside the wheat, "But he said, Nay; lest while ye gather up the tares, ye root up also the wheat with them. Let both grow together until the harvest: and in the time of harvest I will say to the reapers, Gather ye together first the tares, and bind them in bundles to burn them: but gather the wheat into my barn." (Matt. 13:29-30), because we do not know who among us will ultimately choose to be tares, so He asks us to love them all. This is another reason He asks us not to judge others, "Who art thou that judgest another man's servant? to his own master he standeth or falleth. Yea, he shall be holden up: for God is able to make him stand." (Rom. 14:4). When we judge others, we push them away from God's love, effectively pulling them from His garden. He calls us to be part of His family, working to save the ones who want to be saved, "How think ye? if a man have an hundred sheep, and one of them be gone astray, doth he not leave the ninety and nine, and goeth into the mountains, and seeketh that which is gone astray?" (Matt. 18:12). Showing them God's unselfish love is the best way.

God asks us to love as He does, which means we love Him more than we love ourselves and put no other gods before Him, "Thou shalt have no other gods before me." (Ex. 20:3), as He has set no other people before us. His love is unconditional, "For I am persuaded, that neither death, nor life, nor angels, nor principalities, nor powers, nor things present, nor things to come, Nor height, nor depth, nor any other creature, shall be able to separate us from the love of God, which is in Christ Jesus our Lord." (Rom. 8:38-39). He wants us to love Him and everyone else unconditionally. If we refuse to love Him, how will we ever find the path to eternity?

The alternate choice is the horror of eternal separation from God, which Jesus expressed on the cross, "And about the ninth hour Jesus cried with a loud voice, saying, Eli, Eli, lama sabachthani? that is to say, My God, my God, why hast thou forsaken me?" (Matt. 27:46). He wants us to understand nothing in this world comes close to the pain of eternal separation from God. The story of Oscar Wilde's deathbed conversion, whether true or not, forces us to deal with the question we must all face; "will we choose to remain separated from God or become part of His eternal family?" Many of us, like Wilde, will finally face this decision on our deathbeds. How do we benefit from waiting?

Watching the movie "The Passion of Christ" was very painful, for it took me past the intellectual misinformation of that moment into the world of feeling Christ's pain, as I felt Him reach in and grab my heart. It begs the question, "would I take His place on that cross?" Seeing Jesus's life slowly draining from Him on that cross demands a decision. It startled me into realizing just how much God loves me and hates sin. The veil of my pride, which stood between His love and my life, was torn, and now I clearly see God's version of reigning; selfless, not selfish. He demonstrated this while hanging on that cross, wearing a crown of thorns, and flooding this world with His love, "Then said Jesus, Father, forgive them; for they know not what they do. And they parted his raiment, and cast lots." (Lk. 23:3). The intensity of that moment destroyed the shield I had built to hide from the reality of His sacrifice. For now, His scars are eternally etched on my mind, and they continually draw me to Him.

His scars have helped me see past my own scars, allowing me to appreciate the story they tell of my journey to Him, "From henceforth let no man trouble me: for I bear in my body the marks of the Lord Jesus." (Gal. 6:17). He bore His scars to save me, and I now willingly accept the scars of a life in pursuit of Him. This is part of my picking up my cross, "And when he had called the people unto him with his disciples also, he said unto them, Whosoever will come after me, let him deny himself, and take up his cross, and follow me." (Mk. 8:34). So, His peace and joy strengthen me enough to bear the pains of this life, allowing me to get out of my own way, for I have always been the biggest obstacle on the path to my own salvation.

We can only be fit for eternity when we fully love Him. He knows we cannot divide our love between Him and anyone or anything else, for then we would not be drawn to Him and eternity, "No man can serve two masters: for either he will hate the one, and love the other; or else he will hold to the one, and despise the other. Ye cannot serve God and mammon." (Matt. 6:24). It is a matter of priorities, and when we put God first, everything else falls into place. Once we decide to follow Him, we cannot look back, "And Jesus said unto him, No man, having put his hand to the plough, and looking back, is fit for the kingdom of God." (Lk. 9:62). God asks us to burn the ships, as Hernán Cortés did when he arrived in the New World in 1519. Cortés sent a clear message to his men; there is no turning back, as God does to us.

He calls us to spread His message of eternal love to the uttermost part of the earth, "And he said unto them, Go ye into all the world, and preach the gospel to every creature." (Mk 16:15). If we choose otherwise, we will be tossed from wave to wave, by the sea of lies being spread by this dysfunctional, chaotic world, "That we henceforth be no more children, tossed to and fro, and carried about with every wind of doctrine, by the sleight of men, and cunning craftiness, whereby they lie in wait to deceive; But speaking the truth in love, may grow up into him in all things, which is the head, even Christ:" (Eph. 4:14-15). However, Jesus has carved a way through those lies to His salvation. And it is fully explained in the Bible.

God describes His love to help us understand it is selfless, and living selflessly is the only way to thrive within the laws His creation obeys. He is willing to expose the lies of this world to bring us the truth if we would only honestly seek it, "But seek ye first the kingdom of God, and his righteousness; and all these things shall be added unto you." (Matt. 6:33). If I chose to let go of an egg I was holding, it would fall to the ground and break. God did not cause that egg to break. He just set up the laws His creation would obey. When I chose to drop the egg, I decided to rebel against the law of gravity, ending in the destruction of the egg. When we choose to rebel against what God tells us about love, we cannot blame Him for the destruction that follows. He has told us. His love is selfless. We just need to hold on to our egg of selfless love instead of dropping it.

We keep trying to deny His existence in the face of the fact that the more we learn about His creation, the more we discover we do not know, like, gravity and DNA. Trying to use science to deny the existence of God testifies to the fact we are ignoring the proof He has already placed before us, "For the invisible things of him from the creation of the world are clearly seen, being understood by the things that are made, even his eternal power and Godhead; so that they are without excuse." (Rom. 1:20). Only God could create the billions of galaxies in space and the trillions of amazingly diverse cells in the human body.

It is interesting to note that scientists understand the mathematics behind the law of gravity, which allows them to recognize how some parts of His creation physically interact with each other. However, they have been unable to explain what causes it, as they have been unable to explain or demonstrate their theory of life coming from non-life. False science occurs when people use unprovable information to argue for their current beliefs. Unprovable, in scientific terms, means it is unobservable and unrepeatable. None of the lies about evolution are observable and repeatable. This is another example of God's creation obeying Him, our rebellion, and part of the mystery of how He created everything to work together for good. Our disobedience has left us struggling in a dysfunctional world because we refuse to accept the truth, He is our Creator.

The correct path to fully understanding the coding of DNA follows the truth, "Who will have all men to be saved, and to come unto the knowledge of the truth." (1 Tim. 2:4). The truth of DNA is that there are mutations from one generation to the next. However, there has never been a mutation that added information to a genome. Instead, elements are destroyed, information is lost, not gained. When God created Adam and Eve, their DNA was perfect. However, there have been mutations throughout every generation since His creation. Science has recently learned that the human genome follows a process of genetic entropy, which means we are losing parts of God's perfectly created DNA with each generation. Our DNA is decaying, as is the rest of His creation. Before this deterioration reaches a generation unable to reproduce because that part of their DNA no longer functions properly, God will send Jesus to bring us home, "And except those days should be shortened, there should no flesh be saved: but for the elect's sake those days shall be shortened." (Matt. 24:22).

Darwin's finches developed different shaped beaks, leading him to believe they were evolving. Darwin's observations occurred before DNA was discovered. Darwin did not understand that those finches were already capable of changing the shape of their beaks, allowing them to feed on the seeds available in their environment. The coding was stored in their DNA. Those with an agenda attribute these events to evolution. Dr. Lee Spetner, an American physicist with a Ph.D. from MIT, rightfully identifies it as part of the original design. Instead of an example of survival of the fittest, it is an example of innovative design elements being activated, allowing the organism to thrive in an ever-changing environment, "For we are his workmanship, created in Christ Jesus unto good works, which God hath before ordained that we should walk in them." (Eph. 2:10). If God created organisms to live in a wide range of environments, this design would certainly be the most efficient way for them to thrive. This is creation doing what it was designed to do, not evolution. The idea of evolution is just man rebelling against God.

To help us understand that God's original design was perfect and is now deteriorating, instead of evolving, we will take a look at one example of adaption, not evolution, in that original design. When DNA was discovered, we began the process of studying the incredibly complicated systems that allow our bodies to adapt and survive. One of those systems is our immune system. Our B cells and T cells are part of that system. When bacteria or viruses enter the body, the immune system attacks them, breaks them down, and sends their structural information to the B and T cells. These cells can then identify ten or twenty of the more than a trillion types of antibodies they can produce, which have the best chance of defeating the invader. Then those cells produce millions of the most effective antibodies. So instead of storing millions of cells of trillions of types of antibodies, the B and T cells act as manufacturing plants for the specific antibodies needed at the time, a form of just-in-time manufacturing.

Each generation has seen a breakdown in this process, as mutations continue to decay the system's effectiveness. Over the past 50 years, we have had many medical breakthroughs, learned about healthy diets and the need for exercise. By now, life expectancies should be nearing 100. But, instead, we find ourselves battling to get over 80. This is because this life is not the goal, it is a period designed to allow us to choose our eternal fate, and this period in God's plan is nearing an end.

It is our pride that keeps us from reasoning with God, from choosing Jesus, and it leads us to pretend we are gods, which is impossible for He has no equal, "I am the Lord, and there is none else, there is no God beside me: I girded thee, though thou hast not known me:" (Isa. 45:5). And every evil we witness in this life could have been prevented if everyone had followed God's law of love, which is what heaven will be like. This further demonstrates that all things are possible with God when we abide in Him, "But Jesus beheld them, and said unto them, With men this is impossible; but with God all things are possible." (Matt. 19:26), for when we are abiding in His love, we become humble and focus on the needs of others, leading us to love everyone, all of the time.

CHAPTER 6
God Only Wants Us to Reason

"Our world is not divided by race, color, gender, or religion. Our world is divided into wise people and fools. And the fools divide themselves by race, color, gender, or religion." - Nelson Mandela. Proving this statement requires our reasoning, and God is ready to reason when we are, "Come now, and let us reason together, saith the Lord: though your sins be as scarlet, they shall be as white as snow; though they be red like crimson, they shall be as wool." (Isa. 1:18), because He knows our honest reasoning will provide the answers to all of our questions, eventually leading us to believe in Him. Those who know God know He never changes, but our reasoning always leads us to change, for none of us are perfect. We learn the truth of God's existence, His great love for us, and then choose to join Him in the creation of His family. Of course, it is not God who is dividing us into small groups. However, He allows us to foolishly divide ourselves, "Now I beseech you, brethren, mark them which cause divisions and offences contrary to the doctrine which ye have learned; and avoid them." (Jn. 10:9-10).

Reasoning with God leads us to accept Jesus as our Savior, "I am the door: by me if any man enter in, he shall be saved, and shall go in and out, and find pasture. The thief cometh not, but for to steal, and to kill, and to destroy: I am come that they might have life, and that they might have it more abundantly." (Jn. 10:9-10), a bold statement. However, reasoning with Him requires patience, as we allow God to prove He is our Savior, "Wait on the Lord: be of good courage, and he shall strengthen thine heart: wait, I say, on the Lord." (Ps. 27:14), and "To every thing there is a season, and a time to every purpose under the heaven:" (Eccl. 3:1), and "But they that wait upon the Lord shall renew their strength; they shall mount up with wings as eagles; they shall run, and not be weary; and they shall walk, and not faint." (Isa. 40:31). If we refuse to open our minds, we will not be patient enough to reason with our perceived conflicts in His Word before others use them to lure us away from God's love.

We can create all kinds of excuses for not reasoning with His Word, for not believing in Him. Many cite the hypocrites in our society, claiming to be Christians, as the reason for our apathy. Jesus witnessed the same problem with the religious leaders of His day. Our claiming someone else's rebellion prevents us from reasoning with God's truth is only an excuse. What we are really saying is, depart from us, we do not want to know your ways, "Therefore they say unto God, Depart from us; for we desire not the knowledge of thy ways." (Job 21:14), and all of our excuses are merely hollow attempts to somehow justify our willful ignorance. We have chosen to fill our days with activities, leaving us little time to think about God. We spend more time planning a vacation than planning our eternal future. It is a choice, "This I say therefore, and testify in the Lord, that ye henceforth walk not as other Gentiles walk, in the vanity of their mind, Having the understanding darkened, being alienated from the life of God through the ignorance that is in them, because of the blindness of their heart." (Eph. 4:17-18). Our willful ignorance will not save us, "He that rejecteth me, and receiveth not my words, hath one that judgeth him: the word that I have spoken, the same shall judge him in the last day" (Jn. 12:48), for we will have already sentenced ourselves to this life only, giving up the eternal life He invites us to enjoy.

Reasoning with His Word tears the veil of our ignorance and frees us to see the truth, rather than the lies people tell, "Then said Jesus to those Jews which believed on him, If ye continue in my word, then are ye my disciples indeed; And ye shall know the truth, and the truth shall make you free." (Jn. 8:31-32), allowing us to make better decisions. If we read just five pages a day, we will finish the Bible in a year. The year will pass, whether we read those five pages or not. Do we not owe it to ourselves to at least peak past the veil?

Those unwilling to reason with the Bible will never understand it. The truth within will seem like foolishness, "The heart of him that hath understanding seeketh knowledge: but the mouth of fools feedeth on foolishness." (Prov. 15:14). Without consistent feeding, our souls become the stony places, which futilely receives the seed of His Word, "But he that received the seed into stony places, the same is he that heareth the word, and anon with joy receiveth it; Yet hath he not root in himself, but dureth for a while: for when tribulation or persecution ariseth because of the word, by and by he is offended." (Matt. 13:20-21), but, with consistent feeding, we will find the treasure God has left for us, "But the wisdom that is from above is first pure, then peaceable, gentle, and easy to be intreated, full of mercy and good fruits, without partiality, and without hypocrisy." (Jam. 3:17).

Reasoning with our Creator initiates the transformation process, which leads us to His eternal family, "And be not conformed to this world: but be ye transformed by the renewing of your mind, that ye may prove what is that good, and acceptable, and perfect, will of God." (Rom. 12:2). He calls this transformation process sanctification. We begin as seekers, trying to find the truth, and we discover the Bible is God's truth revealed, "All scripture is given by inspiration of God, and is profitable for doctrine, for reproof, for correction, for instruction in righteousness:" (2 Tim. 3:16).

When we reason with the Bible, we learn who Jesus is. Initially, our new knowledge puffs us up, and we become arrogant, thinking we know it all, but God tells us we are feeding on milk because we are not ready for the meat of His Word, which is the deeper meaning hidden therein, "For when for the time ye ought to be teachers, ye have need that one teach you again which be the first principles of the oracles of God; and are become such as have need of milk, and not of strong meat. For every one that useth milk is unskilful in the word of righteousness: for he is a babe. But strong meat belongeth to them that are of full age, even those who by reason of use have their senses exercised to discern both good and evil." (Heb. 5:12-14). We use our immature knowledge to condemn others for their sins by pointing our self-righteous fingers, and God corrects us, "Judge not, and ye shall not be judged: condemn not, and ye shall not be condemned: forgive, and ye shall be forgiven:" (Lk. 6:37).

When God was ready for Jesus to begin His ministry, God made it clear to all humble enough to hear, "And Jesus, when he was baptized, went up straightway out of the water: and, lo, the heavens were opened unto him, and he saw the Spirit of God descending like a dove, and lighting upon him: And lo a voice from heaven, saying, This is my beloved Son, in whom I am well pleased." (Matt. 3:16-17).

Before Jesus came, we were all dead in our sins, "For all have sinned, and come short of the glory of God." (Rom. 3:23). Sure, people sacrificed spotless lambs in hopes of atoning for their sins. However, those sacrifices were only God's foreshadowing Jesus's first appearance because we had hardened our hearts to His law of love. God never wanted our sacrifices. He only wants us to surrender our hearts to Him by believing Jesus is our Savior. Ultimately, He wants us to show the same mercy He has shown us, "For I desired mercy, and not sacrifice; and the knowledge of God more than burnt offerings." (Hos. 6:6), and "But if ye had known what this meaneth, I will have mercy, and not sacrifice, ye would not have condemned the guiltless." (Matt. 12:7).

When we set up our own rituals and worship them rather than God, we are left with burnt offerings and the symbols of religion, "Wherewith shall I come before the Lord, and bow myself before the high God? shall I come before him with burnt offerings, with calves of a year old? Will the Lord be pleased with thousands of rams, or with ten thousands of rivers of oil? shall I give my firstborn for my transgression, the fruit of my body for the sin of my soul? He hath shewed thee, O man, what is good; and what doth the Lord require of thee, but to do justly, and to love mercy, and to walk humbly with thy God?" (Mic. 6:6-8), He wants us to humbly offer mercy to everyone. Unfortunately, most of us hide our conscious thoughts from the pain our sins cause. The pain is still there. We just want to ignore it because we would rather deal with the pain and continue sinning than accept His selfless love. And so, today, we witness an ever-increasing use of drugs to help us mask our pain.

Jesus came to free us from this illusion of unbreakable chains binding us to an endless cycle of sin. We are not slaves to our sins but rather willing participants who choose bondage by refusing to abide in Jesus. We thus free our appetites to reign in the flesh. When we abide in Jesus, our spirit reigns, freeing us from the flesh and the sin we have allowed into our lives, "For the flesh lusteth against the Spirit, and the Spirit against the flesh: and these are contrary the one to the other: so that ye cannot do the things that ye would." (Gal. 5:17).

Freedom from the chains of bondage does not mean we sin no more. It means we no longer try to hide our sins. We are no longer willing participants pretending we are already good enough and do not need saving. After confessing our sins, we sorrow unto Godly repentance and look for ways of preventing those sins in the future, "For godly sorrow worketh repentance to salvation not to be repented of: but the sorrow of the world worketh death." (2 Cor. 7:10). He calls us to progress since He knows we cannot reach perfection on our own. Paul describes the internal battle we all face, "For that which I do I allow not: for what I would, that do I not; but what I hate, that do I." (Rom. 7:15).

"Go ye therefore, and teach all nations, baptizing them in the name of the Father, and of the Son, and of the Holy Ghost:" (Matt. 28:19). God asks us to spread His Word but warns us not to preach another gospel, only the one Jesus brought us, for anything else leads to divisions, "Now I beseech you, brethren, by the name of our Lord Jesus Christ, that ye all speak the same thing, and that there be no divisions among you; but that ye be perfectly joined together in the same mind and in the same judgment. For it hath been declared unto me of you, my brethren, by them which are of the house of Chloe, that there are contentions among you. Now this I say, that every one of you saith, I am of Paul; and I of Apollos; and I of Cephas; and I of Christ. Is Christ divided? was Paul crucified for you? or were ye baptized in the name of Paul?" (1 Cor. 1:10-13). Is Jesus divided? Where do we find Jesus telling us His church should be divided?

Why would we follow any other voice? "But Peter and John answered and said unto them, Whether it be right in the sight of God to hearken unto you more than unto God, judge ye." (Acts 4:19). Instead of dividing ourselves into denominations, we should be working to unite into one church, His church, fully following His law of love. There were no denominations in the first-century church, and there are no denominations today in the Christian church in Iran. God calls us to get out of our heads and begin living His law of love instead of wasting our energy dividing His church.

When we believers have different interpretations of scripture, we can listen to each other. Then we can consider the new information, which helps us understand how the other person's reasoning led them to their interpretation. Next, keeping every verse in context; chapter, book, and the whole Bible, remembering that there can be no conflicts in His Word, and using the discernment of the Holy Ghost, we each must decide for ourselves, "Where is the wise? where is the scribe? where is the disputer of this world? hath not God made foolish the wisdom of this world? For after that in the wisdom of God the world by wisdom knew not God, it pleased God by the foolishness of preaching to save them that believe." (1 Cor. 1:20-21). We are not to judge others and their beliefs. Instead, we are to help each other, as iron sharpens iron, "Iron sharpeneth iron; so a man sharpeneth the countenance of his friend." (Prov. 27:17). We will all know the truth when we get to heaven.

We are all supposed to work together through the sanctification process to a better understanding of God's Word, "Of these things put them in remembrance, charging them before the Lord that they strive not about words to no profit, but to the subverting of the hearers. Study to shew thyself approved unto God, a workman that needeth not to be ashamed, rightly dividing the word of truth." (2 Tim. 2:14-15), and "But foolish and unlearned questions avoid, knowing that they do gender strifes. And the servant of the Lord must not strive; but be gentle unto all men, apt to teach, patient, In meekness instructing those that oppose themselves; if God peradventure will give them repentance to the acknowledging of the truth;" (2 Tim. 2:23-25), and "But avoid foolish questions, and genealogies, and contentions, and strivings about the law; for they are unprofitable and vain." (Tit. 3:9). We are then to preach Christ, in love, and let the Holy Ghost do His job, "What then? notwithstanding, every way, whether in pretence, or in truth, Christ is preached; and I therein do rejoice, yea, and will rejoice." (Phil. 1:18). Most importantly, we are called to actively live God's law of love.

Does the Holy Ghost need our help? As we grow in the Bible's knowledge, some of us continue pointing our self-righteousness fingers to judge the wounded. Are we helping the Holy Ghost, or are we becoming stumbling blocks? God has harsh words for those of us who choose to become stumbling blocks, "I will consume man and beast; I will consume the fowls of the heaven, and the fishes of the sea, and the stumbling blocks with the wicked: and I will cut off man from off the land, saith the Lord." (Zeph. 1:3). God's Word is our spiritual mirror, which each of us can use to aid us in our own transformation. Our job is to love others, thus reflecting God's love, "If ye fulfil the royal law according to the scripture, Thou shalt love thy neighbour as thyself, ye do well." (Jam. 2:8), as the early Christians did. When we demonstrate God's selfless love, others are drawn to reason with Him. So then, the Holy Ghost can hold our individual spiritual mirror for us to witness our own sins when we are ready to reason with them.

If we turn our spiritual mirror onto others, we illustrate our misunderstanding of God's plan, for God has clearly told us the Holy Ghost does not need our help and we should not judge others, for we were never meant to cut down people in God's name, "Judge not, that ye be not judged. For with what judgment ye judge, ye shall be judged: and with what measure ye mete, it shall be measured to you again. And why beholdest thou the mote that is in thy brother's eye, but considerest not the beam that is in thine own eye? Or how wilt thou say to thy brother, Let me pull out the mote out of thine eye; and, behold, a beam is in thine own eye? Thou hypocrite, first cast out the beam out of thine own eye; and then shalt thou see clearly to cast out the mote out of thy brother's eye." (Matt. 7:1-5), and since we are not perfect, "For there is not a just man upon earth, that doeth good, and sinneth not." (Eccl. 7:20), those we accuse with our self-righteousness see us as hypocrites, driving them away from God instead of drawing them to Him.

God does call us to help introduce Him to others, which is why He wants us to be ready to give an answer, "But sanctify the Lord God in your hearts: and be ready always to give an answer to every man that asketh you a reason of the hope that is in you with meekness and fear:" (1 Pet. 3:15). Being ready to answer questions is not the same as walking around, pointing our fingers at people, and telling them how they need to change. Instead, we must wait for their questions, which shows they are interested in reasoning with God. We can never justify pointing our fingers at others. And, what does it say about our own lives? "So when they continued asking him, he lifted up himself, and said unto them, He that is without sin among you, let him first cast a stone at her." (Jn. 8:7). Are we fully living God's law of love? Or, are we picking up our stones instead of showing others God's love and forgiveness? We are all on different parts of the path to God, and we never know whether another person is ahead of us or behind us. Do we really want to be judged before we have had every opportunity to understand the choice before us? We can learn from the religious leaders of Jesus's time. The scribes were self-righteous and thought they were God's chosen people. However, Jesus thought otherwise, "Beware of the scribes, which desire to walk in long robes, and love greetings in the markets, and the highest seats in the synagogues, and the chief rooms at feasts; Which devour widows' houses, and for a shew make long prayers: the same shall receive greater damnation." (Lk. 20:46-47).

Reasoning requires us to study the whole Bible, not just a few selected verses. To do this, we must come to His Word with an open mind. Otherwise, we will respond with hostility, angrily crying, "no matter what you say, I will not believe." This is what we witness as the Pharisees came to question Jesus, having no interest in learning, only in trapping Jesus into saying something they could use against Him, "Then went the Pharisees, and took counsel how they might entangle him in his talk … But Jesus perceived their wickedness, and said, Why tempt ye me, ye hypocrites? … And no man was able to answer him a word, neither durst any man from that day forth ask him any more questions." (Matt. 22:15, 18, 46). Of course, they failed miserably.

Ultimately, there can be no conflicts in God's Word, and if we think we are reading something that contradicts another part of the Bible, we misunderstand one, or both, of those messages from God. When we honestly reason with Him, we witness those perceived conflicts dissolve in the warm waters of His love. But, of course, living under the law of love, we must also allow others the same freedom, without judging them or their current opinions. I can testify that when I have opened my mind to different opinions, willingly reasoning rather than being closed to new ideas, I have grown in the knowledge of our Lord. We all have the same amount of time each day and suffer from the same ailment of procrastination. Therefore, only those who proactively allocate time to reason with God will actually do it.

CHAPTER 7
The Bible

The Bible is a collection of sixty-six books written by some forty authors over 1,500 years. Nothing less than a miracle could cause forty writers spread over 1,500 years to write such a cohesive work. Only God could inspire this work, "All scripture is given by inspiration of God, and is profitable for doctrine, for reproof, for correction, for instruction in righteousness: That the man of God may be perfect, thoroughly furnished unto all good works." (2 Tim. 3:16-17). He asks each of us to reason with His Word for ourselves, "Study to shew thyself approved unto God, a workman that needeth not to be ashamed, rightly dividing the word of truth." (2 Tim. 2:15). God wants us to challenge everything we read and hear, including what we think we read in the Bible, "Beloved, believe not every spirit, but try the spirits whether they are of God: because many false prophets are gone out into the world." (1 Jn. 4:1), and "Prove all things; hold fast that which is good." (1 Thess. 5:21). Every verse in the Bible teaches us something about God, His love, and our rebellion.

The Bible is not a list of dos and don'ts; it is God describing His law of love and our rebellion. It is humanity that keeps making up lists of dos and don'ts. We are the ones rebelling against God's simple law of love, and we keep trying to get others to do what we want them to do. God gave us the Bible to help us understand the difference between loving unconditionally and trying to force others to love us, or worse, obey us because we want to be their god. The Bible teaches us how to become humble and unselfish, to care for others more than we care for ourselves, "This is my commandment, That ye love one another, as I have loved you." (Jn. 15:12). If we do not understand God's unselfish law of love, how will we ever choose to live it?

Wait … Didn't God give us the Ten Commandments and all of the Mosaic Laws? Aren't there 613 laws in the Torah? It appears so, but are they all really from God? Not exactly. Because we would not accept His simple law of love, God had Moses bring us the Ten Commandments (Ex. 20:2-17) and Jesus the beatitudes (Matt. 5:1-48), and we have responded by hardening our hearts and creating an uncountable number of unnecessary laws. Those who produce these unnecessary laws want us to feel like a society of lawbreakers, which generates a hostile atmosphere of fear, guilt, and foreboding. Then they layer in the idea of scarcity to heighten societal anxiety. The laws we have created are not intended to save us, only to control us. Those trying to control us want us to think we are running out of water, air quality is eroding, and we are losing our ability to protect ourselves from viruses and people who wish to harm us. These illusions weaken our resolve and leave us with feelings of fear and helplessness. Then they purport themselves to be the answer, which only leads us away from God's path to eternity.

God's law of love is all we need, and when we are living it, we become selfless; giving and sharing, which produces an attitude of peace and plenty, and results in the fruit of an ever-increasing number of good works pouring out of us, "For we are his workmanship, created in Christ Jesus unto good works, which God hath before ordained that we should walk in them." (Eph. 2:10). This is how His law of love shines His light, drawing others to Him, "And let us consider one another to provoke unto love and to good works." (Heb. 10:24). We can have this attitude of plenty because God will provide for all of our needs, "But my God shall supply all your need according to his riches in glory by Christ Jesus." (Phil. 4:19).

He established a covenant with us long before we hardened our hearts and began creating our own laws, many of which we attribute to God, "But with thee will I establish my covenant; and thou shalt come into the ark, thou, and thy sons, and thy wife, and thy sons' wives with thee." (Gen. 6:18). His covenant relationship, like the marriage vow, is founded on a promise of love, "Know therefore that the Lord thy God, he is God, the faithful God, which keepeth covenant and mercy with them that love him and keep his commandments to a thousand generations." (Deut. 7:9). His promises are for everyone who chooses to accept His love because He already loves every one of us, "And this is the will of him that sent me, that every one which seeth the Son, and believeth on him, may have everlasting life: and I will raise him up at the last day." (Jn. 6:40). He didn't say God loves every Jew; He said "every one" and He created us to live with Him.

In Matthew, Jesus helps us understand how the hardening of our hearts leads us away from His love and toward the creation of our own laws, many of which we attribute to God, such as divorce, "They say unto him, Why did Moses then command to give a writing of divorcement, and to put her away? He saith unto them, Moses because of the hardness of your hearts suffered you to put away your wives: but from the beginning it was not so." (Matt. 19:7-8). **Notice He said that "Moses suffered you," not God, and "from the beginning it was not so."** There was no divorce in the garden, it is not part of the Ten Commandments, and it has no place in God's law of love. In Mark, Jesus tells us we have chosen to teach the doctrines of men, including the 613 Mitzvot of the Torah rather than His simple commandment of love, "Howbeit in vain do they worship me, teaching for doctrines the commandments of men. For laying aside the commandment of God, ye hold the tradition of men, as the washing of pots and cups: and many other such like things ye do. And he said unto them, Full well ye reject the commandment of God, that ye may keep your own tradition." (Mk. 7:7-9). **Notice He said, "laying aside the commandment of God," commandment, not commandments.** We do not need the 613 commandments in the Torah, many of which we have created, if we live His law of love because He does not care how we wash our pots, only how we love each other.

Of the 613 commandments, only those describing God's law of love are important to Him. He does not want us to set up lists of things people should or should not do, for those lists would oppose God's law of love and push people away from Him. Instead, God keeps it simple; we are to love everyone all of the time, "Owe no man any thing, but to love one another: for he that loveth another hath fulfilled the law." (Rom. 13:8). **This means that we are to live His law of love all of the time and not try to force it on others.** Instead, we are to reflect His light, "But if we walk in the light, as he is in the light, we have fellowship one with another, and the blood of Jesus Christ his Son cleanseth us from all sin." (1 Jn. 1:7). **His light draws others to Him if they are ready to accept His love.**

We are to love everyone and forgive their sins, "Take heed to yourselves: If thy brother trespass against thee, rebuke him; and if he repent, forgive him. And if he trespass against thee seven times in a day, and seven times in a day turn again to thee, saying, I repent; thou shalt forgive him." (Lk. 17:3-4), **no matter what the consequences are.** This is part of picking up our cross, which draws people to Him, "And he said to them all, If any man will come after me, let him deny himself, and take up his cross daily, and follow me." (Lk. 9:23). **For we would be reflecting His love and selflessness.**

God wants us to read the whole Bible, so we can see how it all fits together and help us understand the truth of His will for us, "For this cause we also, since the day we heard it, do not cease to pray for you, and to desire that ye might be filled with the knowledge of his will in all wisdom and spiritual understanding." (Col. 1:9). He continues to protect His Word from those who would change it or attempt to keep the rest of us from understanding it, "The words of the Lord are pure words: as silver tried in a furnace of earth, purified seven times. Thou shalt keep them, O Lord, thou shalt preserve them from this generation for ever." (Ps. 12:6-7).

This is why God called a wealthy merchant, Peter Waldo, to give up his property in 1173 to create the Poor Men of Lyon. They would come to be called the Waldensians, and they dedicated their lives to distributing handwritten copies of parts of the Bible translated into local languages. But, unfortunately, the church leaders were prohibiting the translation of the Bible because they were busy adding burdens to the common man's life. Moreover, these church leaders hated the Waldensians for challenging the church's departure from scripture.

And as part of the Inquisition initiated by Pope Lucius III in 1184, the church branded the Waldensians heretics and began hunting down these soldiers of God, killing thousands of them. One day, the church trapped 3,000 Waldensians in a cave, built a fire at the cave entrance, and suffocated them. Did the church's response to the Waldensians demonstrate God's law of love? No matter how treacherous the church became or how many they tortured and killed, they could not keep God's people from doing His work. Can we not see we were all made to be courageous? "Only let your conversation be as it becometh the gospel of Christ: that whether I come and see you, or else be absent, I may hear of your affairs, that ye stand fast in one spirit, with one mind striving together for the faith of the gospel; And in nothing terrified by your adversaries: which is to them an evident token of perdition, but to you of salvation, and that of God." (Phil. 1:27-28), and "For God hath not given us the spirit of fear; but of power, and of love, and of a sound mind." (2 Tim. 1:9). We are to preach the gospel and lead others to our risen Lord.

"And I saw a new heaven and a new earth: for the first heaven and the first earth were passed away; and there was no more sea. And I John saw the holy city, new Jerusalem, coming down from God out of heaven, prepared as a bride adorned for her husband. And I heard a great voice out of heaven saying, Behold, the tabernacle of God is with men, and he will dwell with them, and they shall be his people, and God himself shall be with them, and be their God." (Rev. 21:1-3). Those who have lied and changed His Word or the meaning of His Word will not be part of His family, "For I testify unto every man that heareth the words of the prophecy of this book, If any man shall add unto these things, God shall add unto him the plagues that are written in this book: And if any man shall take away from the words of the book of this prophecy, God shall take away his part out of the book of life, and out of the holy city, and from the things which are written in this book." (Rev 22:18-19). There can be no other way, for only those who genuinely love Him and His Word will be fit to live together for all eternity within a family totally in love with each other.

God knows the number of people He wants in His family, and even though He would like all of us to accept His offer, He knows only a percentage of us will. So, He uses these two numbers to calculate how many people He needs to create and the date He will send Jesus back to us. Those of us who choose to accept His offer will be taken to heaven. This is what guarantees there will be no pain and suffering in heaven, "And God shall wipe away all tears from their eyes; and there shall be no more death, neither sorrow, nor crying, neither shall there be any more pain: for the former things are passed away." (Rev. 21:4). If we want to be in heaven, we need to come to His Word and reason with it for ourselves; this is the only way we will ever get past this world's lies and finally understand His unselfish law of love.

God wants us to understand that the Ten Commandments are nothing more than a clarification of His law of love in a few areas of our lives. As an example, Moses pointed to God's love by giving us the short version on the subject of killing in Exodus, "Thou shalt not kill," (Ex. 20:13), but in the Be-Attitudes, Jesus went deeper, "Ye have heard that it was said of them of old time, Thou shalt not kill; and whosoever shall kill shall be in danger of the judgment: But I say unto you, That whosoever is angry with his brother without a cause shall be in danger of the judgment: and whosoever shall say to his brother, Raca, shall be in danger of the council: but whosoever shall say, Thou fool, shall be in danger of hell fire." (Matt. 5:21-22). Being angry with our brother means we are judging, and it will not lead to our forgiveness.

If we want to understand whether a commandment is from God, we need only use the plumb line of God's law of love as Jesus did when He summarized the Ten Commandments, "Jesus said unto him,

51

Thou shalt love the Lord thy God with all thy heart, and with all thy soul, and with all thy mind. This is the first and great commandment." (Matt. 22:37-38). That was a summary of the first four of the ten. "And the second is like unto it, Thou shalt love thy neighbour as thyself. On these two commandments hang all the law and the prophets." (Matt. 22:39-40), and this was a summary of the final six. Together, these four verses provide the foundation of God's law of love. God brought us this truth before He sent Jesus to reaffirm it, "And thou shalt love the Lord thy God with all thine heart, and with all thy soul, and with all thy might." (Deut. 6:5), and "But the stranger that dwelleth with you shall be unto you as one born among you, and thou shalt love him as thyself; for ye were strangers in the land of Egypt: I am the Lord your God." (Lev. 19:34). God never changes, and those who would have us believe He does are lying to us.

Until we realize Jesus came to help us understand God's Word, we will be lost in Pharisee-like interpretations arguing about the meaning behind the original Greek and Hebrew words, the correct number of books the Bible should include, or debating the 613 commandments in the Torah. "And they were all amazed and marvelled, saying one to another, Behold, are not all these which speak Galilaeans? And how hear we every man in our own tongue, wherein we were born?" (Acts 2:7-8). Thus, God tells us His Word will be delivered in every language to the uttermost part of the earth. We are being drawn to Him by His unselfish love and the fulfilling of His prophecies, "But in the last days it shall come to pass, that the mountain of the house of the Lord shall be established in the top of the mountains, and it shall be exalted above the hills; and people shall flow unto it. And many nations shall come, and say, Come, and let us go up to the mountain of the Lord, and to the house of the God of Jacob; and he will teach us of his ways, and we will walk in his paths: for the law shall go forth of Zion, and the word of the Lord from Jerusalem." (Mic. 4:1-2), and "And it shall come to pass in the last days, that the mountain of the Lord's house shall be established in the top of the mountains, and shall be exalted above the hills; and all nations shall flow unto it. And many people shall go and say, Come ye, and let us go up to the mountain of the Lord, to the house of the God of Jacob; and he will teach us of his ways, and we will walk in his paths: for out of Zion shall go forth the law, and the word of the Lord from Jerusalem." (Isa. 2:2-3). Eventually, we will understand His Word, God does not mumble, and our language is no barrier, for His law of love transcends language, "In meekness instructing those that oppose themselves; if God peradventure will give them repentance to the acknowledging of the truth; And that they may recover themselves out of the snare of the devil, who are taken captive by him at his will." (2 Tim. 2:25-26).

His Word will soon be heard in the uttermost part of the earth fulfilling those prophecies, and He asks us not to argue about differing interpretations or translations, "But foolish and unlearned questions avoid, knowing that they do gender strifes. And the servant of the Lord must not strive; but be gentle unto all men, apt to teach, patient." (2 Tim. 2:23-24). All we need to do is use the plumb line of God's law of love and make sure there are no conflicts in our individual interpretation of His meaning. It is like working on a jigsaw puzzle. Two pieces cannot fit in the same place, and two verses in God's Word cannot have contradictory meanings. Instead, there is one consistent meaning throughout the Bible. The apparent conflicts in the Bible have all been exposed to be nothing more than our rebellion.

Jesus tells us killing our brother is not an act of love, and neither is being angry with him. Every law humanity has created, including those we have attributed to God, are examples of God allowing us to harden our hearts unto our own death. If we truly loved our neighbors, we would not kill them. Thus, if everyone lived God's law of love as they will in heaven, there would be no need for laws to punish those who kill because there would be no killers. We can use this same thought process to see how everything evil would disappear if we all lived His law of love. Once we see that the apparent conflicts in His Word are caused by people distorting God's law of love, we can spread His truth to everyone.

So, the Bible is God's love letter to us. It explains His law of love, the fact that His love is unconditional, and that He will not force us to love Him. This is why He asks us to reason with His Word for ourselves until we settle the issue of our belief in our own hearts and minds, which will lead us to Jesus, "For I delivered unto you first of all that which I also received, how that Christ died for our sins according to the scriptures;" (1 Cor. 15:3-4). Then we can understand why Jesus asks us to repent, "From that time Jesus began to preach, and to say, Repent: for the kingdom of heaven is at hand." (Matt. 4:17), we will then share His love, "And he answering said, Thou shalt love the Lord thy God with all thy heart, and with all thy soul, and with all thy strength, and with all thy mind; and thy neighbour as thyself." (Lk. 10:27), and preach His gospel to the uttermost part of the earth, "Go ye therefore, and teach all nations, baptizing them in the name of the Father, and of the Son, and of the Holy Ghost: Teaching them to observe all things whatsoever I have commanded you: and, lo, I am with you always, even unto the end of the world. Amen." (Matt. 28:19-20).

CHAPTER 8
Jesus Then and Now

What does God tell us about Jesus's two appearances?

One of the most critical themes in the Old Testament points to Jesus's first appearance. He came that first time, as the lamb of God and the Old Testament provided over three hundred prophecies about Jesus's first appearance, "Declaring the end from the beginning, and from ancient times the things that are not yet done, saying, My counsel shall stand, and I will do all my pleasure:" (Isa. 46:10), and Jesus told us people would not be persuaded unless they believed Moses and the prophets, "And he said unto him, If they hear not Moses and the prophets, neither will they be persuaded, though one rose from the dead." (Lk. 16:31). God gives us the free will to ignore His prophecies or use them to elevate our faith. He wants us to know He is the eternal King and He came to show us His form of reigning; love, not force, "Rejoice greatly, O daughter of Zion; shout, O daughter of Jerusalem: behold, thy King cometh unto thee: he is just, and having salvation; lowly, and riding upon an ass, and upon a colt the foal of an ass." (Zech. 9:9), and He is patient enough to wait for us to accept His offer. He will not force it upon us.

God's prophecies also emphasize the hardened hearts of the religious leaders, who knew them well and still ignored the fact that Jesus fulfilled all of them. Nevertheless, many who saw Jesus believed, including doubting Thomas, albeit only after seeing the wounds in His resurrected body, "Jesus saith unto him, Thomas, because thou hast seen me, thou hast believed: blessed are they that have not seen, and yet have believed." (Jn. 20:29). However, many others chose to deny the truth Who stood before them, "Jesus answered them, Many good works have I shewed you from my Father; for which of those works do ye stone me? The Jews answered him, saying, For a good work we stone thee not; but for blasphemy; and because that thou, being a man, makest thyself God." (Jn. 10:32-33), even though they witnessed the miracles. He was not making Himself God. He is God. They ignored the prophecies and His works because they did not want to acknowledge He is the Messiah. Those religious leaders thought Jesus had come to expose their made-up laws and to undermine their authority. However, when they chose to deny Jesus's deity, were they not at the same time proving He really existed?

Part of the great mystery of Christ is that so many people choose to deny the truth, even some who witnessed His miracles, His healing power, His resurrections of the dead, and the fact this life is better when we live His law of love, "And when he thus had spoken, he cried with a loud voice, Lazarus, come forth. And he that was dead came forth, bound hand and foot with graveclothes: and his face was bound about with a napkin. Jesus saith unto them, Loose him, and let him go." (Jn. 11:43-44). Many ignore the historical evidence of Jesus's existence and His sacrifice on the cross, even though plenty of non-Christian references from that period are available today. If Jesus is the Messiah, could anything in this life be more important than examining the evidence? Yet mysteriously, people refuse to consider the evidence and accept unfounded rumors instead.

We can all agree that there is a dispute about which names we should use in our calendar; A.D., B.C., B.C.E., or C.E. I have wrestled with this dispute and continue to wonder why removing any reference to God from these names is so important to some people? B.C. was first used because they wanted to distinguish between the period "before Christ" and the A.D. period after He first appeared to us, "Anno Domini" in Latin, or "in the year of our Lord" in English. Both Dionysius Exiguus and Pope Gregory XIII tried to sync the calendar with God's created cycles of the seasons. Their primary purpose was to accurately identify Easter Sunday for future years. Hundreds of years later, during the Age of Enlightenment, a period in which some people were desperately trying to remove God from their lives, produced the replacement names of B.C.E., "Before the Current Era," and C.E., "Current Era." This period also brought us the false narrative of evolution for the same reason. What good has all of our disobedience produced?

When God placed Adam and Eve in the garden, they experienced what life will be like in heaven. Everything worked together perfectly, "And we know that all things work together for good to them that love God, to them who are the called according to his purpose." (Rom. 8:28). Satan then came to

Eve to create doubt. This doubt grew to disobedience, leading both Adam and Eve away from God's perfect creation, as they no longer loved God to obedience, "If ye love me, keep my commandments." (Jn. 14:15) and they had only one commandment to keep. Little did they know that that commandment was the essence of God's law of love, "For all the law is fulfilled in one word, even in this; Thou shalt love thy neighbour as thyself." (Gal. 5:14), for all of the law is fulfilled when we love God.

We can think of this world as our chance to experience both heaven and hell. When we are working together to complete God's family by living His law of love, everything works together to bring us Jesus's peace and everyone benefits from our behavior. This is the convergent space where heaven and earth kiss. When we do not love God, we think everything should work together for our own benefit, selfishness rules our hearts. This is where earth and hell converge to produce pain and suffering. It is our disobedience, foolishly displayed, that turns this world into our temporary hell, causing some of us to take our own lives. We therefore, are deciding our own eternal future by choosing to either obey or disobey God's law of love. And, we cannot love Him or keep His commandments, if we do not believe He exists, "But without faith it is impossible to please him: for he that cometh to God must believe that he is, and that he is a rewarder of them that diligently seek him." (Heb. 11:6).

Because so many deny Jesus is the Son of God, I continually look for proof sources in hopes of being ready to answer the questions people ask about God and the Bible. So, I read "The Resurrection of the Son of God" by N.T. Wright. It is easy to lay down the free will God has given us and accept the lies intended to drive us away from God. However, Wright's book painstakingly takes us through most of the available evidence of Jesus's crucifixion and resurrection. In addition, this book identifies many of the historical references available from non-Christian sources, which adequately prove Jesus walked this earth and died, as the Bible tells us. After reasoning with the evidence, I wondered why I ever doubted what I have always felt deep in my heart, "I was not created to live in this world," there is just too much hatred and strife. Doubt is the devil's disease that leads us away from God to our own death, and Eve was the first one to be infected.

I have since learned; that all the proof I ever needed was available in the Bible. All I had to do was read it, reason with it, and then apply the truths to my daily life to experience the fullness of God's peace and the proof that He changes lives, "Therefore if any man be in Christ, he is a new creature: old things are passed away; behold, all things are become new." (2 Cor. 5:17), He certainly changed mine.

The Bible tells us Jesus was there before time began, "In the beginning was the Word, and the Word was with God, and the Word was God." (Jn. 1:1). He was later born into our world of a woman in Bethlehem, "But thou, Bethlehem Ephratah, though thou be little among the thousands of Judah, yet out of thee shall he come forth unto me that is to be ruler in Israel; whose goings forth have been from of old, from everlasting." (Mic. 5:2). God told us it would be a virgin birth, another miracle to be witnessed, "Therefore the Lord himself shall give you a sign; Behold, a virgin shall conceive, and bear a son, and shall call his name Immanuel." (Isa. 7:14), and Jesus would be the Prince of Peace for all who accept Him as their Savior, "For unto us a child is born, unto us a son is given: and the government shall be upon his shoulder: and his name shall be called Wonderful, Counsellor, The mighty God, The everlasting Father, The Prince of Peace." (Isa. 9:6).

Jesus would come this first time humbly to announce His kingdom, riding upon the colt of an ass to bring us salvation, "Rejoice greatly, O daughter of Zion; shout, O daughter of Jerusalem: behold, thy King cometh unto thee: he is just, and having salvation; lowly, and riding upon an ass, and upon a colt the foal of an ass." (Zech. 9:9).

Jesus spent forty days with His followers, after His resurrection, to leave us plenty of eyewitnesses, proving He had risen and is not some fictional character, "And ye also shall bear witness, because ye have been with me from the beginning." (Jn. 15:27), and "To whom also he shewed himself alive after his passion by many infallible proofs, being seen of them forty days, and speaking of the things pertaining to the kingdom of God … But ye shall receive power, after that the Holy Ghost is come upon you: and ye shall be witnesses unto me both in Jerusalem, and in all Judaea, and in Samaria, and unto the uttermost part of the earth." (Acts 1:3, 8). He is talking about you and me. We do not live in Jerusalem, Judaea, or Samaria; we live in the "uttermost part of the earth." We are the living proof of the continuing progress of Peter's work, assigned to him by Jesus, "This is now the third time that Jesus shewed himself to his disciples, after that he was risen from the dead. So when they had dined, Jesus saith to Simon Peter, Simon, son of Jonas, lovest thou me more than these? He saith unto him, Yea, Lord; thou knowest that I love thee. He saith unto him, Feed my lambs. He saith to him again the second time, Simon, son of Jonas, lovest thou me? He saith unto him, Yea, Lord; thou knowest that I love thee. He saith unto him, Feed my sheep. He saith unto him the third time, Simon, son of Jonas, lovest thou me? Peter was grieved because he said unto him the third time, Lovest thou me? And he said unto him, Lord, thou knowest all things; thou knowest that I love thee. Jesus saith unto him, Feed my sheep." (Jn. 21:14-17).

Jesus came to help us understand Him and the Bible. He fully explained His mission, we cannot pretend He came for any other purpose. "A man who was merely a man and said the sort of things Jesus said would not be a great moral teacher. He would either be a lunatic — on the level with the man who says he is a poached egg — or else he would be the Devil of Hell. You must make your choice. Either this man was, and is, the Son of God, or else a madman or something worse. You can shut him up for a fool, you can spit at him and kill him as a demon or you can fall at his feet and call him Lord and God, but let us not come with any patronizing nonsense about his being a great human teacher. He has not left that open to us. He did not intend to." - C.S. Lewis (Mere Christianity).

We can use His Word and His prophecies to establish our faith, but only when we are drawn to His love will we hear them, "But ye believe not, because ye are not of my sheep, as I said unto you. My sheep hear my voice, and I know them, and they follow me:" (Jn. 10:26-27).

One of the most significant themes in the New Testament points us to Jesus's second coming. He wants us to prepare for eternity, and once we learn God wants to spend eternity with us, we are no longer in a hurry to have our own way, and we can relax and live His selfless law of love.

When Jesus returns, it will be as the Lion of Judah, bringing the host of heaven. A trump shall announce His coming, and those who have chosen to ignore Him will mourn, as they watch those who decided to accept Him rise to meet Him in the sky, "And then shall appear the sign of the Son of man in heaven: and then shall all the tribes of the earth mourn, and they shall see the Son of man coming in the clouds of heaven with power and great glory. And he shall send his angels with a great sound of a trumpet, and they shall gather together his elect from the four winds, from one end of heaven to the other." (Matt. 24:30-31). The trump will sound without warning, there will be no time to change our minds, "For the Lord himself shall descend from heaven with a shout, with the voice of the archangel, and with the trump of God: and the dead in Christ shall rise first: Then we which are alive and remain shall be caught up together with them in the clouds, to meet the Lord in the air: and so shall we ever be with the Lord." (1 Thess. 4:16-17).

It will be like the day Noe entered the ark after 120 years of building it, "For as in the days that were before the flood they were eating and drinking, marrying and giving in marriage, until the day that Noe entered into the ark, And knew not until the flood came, and took them all away; so shall also the coming of the Son of man be." (Matt. 24:38-39). Apparently, 120 years of warnings were not enough for the people of Noe's day. Hopefully, 2,000 years have been enough for us, "In a moment, in the twinkling of an eye, at the last trump: for the trumpet shall sound, and the dead shall be raised incorruptible, and we shall be changed." (1 Cor. 15:52). Every eye will see His return, and many will wail at their loss, "Behold, he cometh with clouds; and every eye shall see him, and they also which pierced him: and all kindreds of the earth shall wail because of him. Even so, Amen." (Rev. 1:7). If Jesus suddenly appeared to us and told us He would be coming back tomorrow, would we believe Him? If we knew Jesus was standing next to us, would it change the way we lived? Would we be kinder and more forgiving? How would we respond to the temptations of this world?

The truth is Jesus is standing next to each of us, "Let your conversation be without covetousness; and be content with such things as ye have: for he hath said, I will never leave thee, nor forsake thee." (Heb. 13:5), and Jesus proved it when He walked in the fire with Shadrach, Meshach, and Abednego, "He answered and said, Lo, I see four men loose, walking in the midst of the fire, and they have no hurt; and the form of the fourth is like the Son of God." (Dan. 3:25). When we surrender to His love, we become a new person, and the works of the devil no longer have a hold over us, "Therefore if any man be in Christ, he is a new creature: old things are passed away; behold, all things are become new." (2 Cor. 5:17).

God has Peter explain the need for us to be patient during these 2,000 years of waiting for Jesus's second coming. God does not want any of us to perish without being given every possible opportunity to change our minds, accept His offer, and repent, as Dustin Higgs did. God waits for each of us to come to Him, like a father waiting for his daughter to come home from her first date. The main difference being this Father already knows who will come home to Him. Can we imagine what the father waiting for his daughter would feel if he already knew she would not return that night? My heart aches at the thought. Yet, this is the pain God feels every time one of us refuses to reason with

His truth. His longsuffering encourages us to have the patience necessary to wait for our Savior's return, as He is waiting for us to complete His family. The judgment awaits all; however, only those who willingly accept Jesus as our Savior will be saved, "The Lord is not slack concerning his promise, as some men count slackness; but is longsuffering to us-ward, not willing that any should perish, but that all should come to repentance. But the day of the Lord will come as a thief in the night; in the which the heavens shall pass away with a great noise, and the elements shall melt with fervent heat, the earth also and the works that are therein shall be burned up." (2 Pet. 3:9-10).

When we step before our Lord and Savior, on the day of judgment, we will either hear, "His lord said unto him, Well done, good and faithful servant; thou hast been faithful over a few things, I will make thee ruler over many things: enter thou into the joy of thy lord." (Matt. 25:23) or "And then will I profess unto them, I never knew you: depart from me, ye that work iniquity." (Matt. 7:23). In this life, we will choose which of these two greetings we will receive. Jesus wants all of us to choose to be with Him forever; however, He will not force any of us to love Him, "Say unto them, As I live, saith the Lord God, I have no pleasure in the death of the wicked; but that the wicked turn from his way and live: turn ye, turn ye from your evil ways; for why will ye die, O house of Israel?" (Eze. 33:11).

Jesus did not die on the cross and ascend from the grave for no reason. These two events are the most profound moments in all human history. The reason for them is no less profound; He did these things so that we might have a choice. God wants us to know He resurrected Jesus. He desires to do the same for us, "And God hath both raised up the Lord, and will also raise up us by his own power." (1 Cor. 6:14). Otherwise, we have only the hopelessness that has led so many of us to take our own lives because we no longer want to live in this world. Unfortunately, some of us will choose to live selfish lives, defiantly demonstrating our separation from God, "But your iniquities have separated between you and your God, and your sins have hid his face from you, that he will not hear." (Isa. 59:2).

So, what is Jesus doing now? He is preparing a place for each of us in His Father's house, "Let not your heart be troubled: ye believe in God, believe also in me. In my Father's house are many mansions: if it were not so, I would have told you. I go to prepare a place for you. And if I go and prepare a place for you, I will come again, and receive you unto myself; that where I am, there ye may be also." (Jn. 14:1-3).

He is holding His creation together, "And he is before all things, and by him all things consist." (Col. 1:17), and "In whom also we have obtained an inheritance, being predestinated according to the purpose of him who worketh all things after the counsel of his own will:" (Eph. 1:11). And He has shortened this earth's history, "And except those days should be shortened, there should no flesh be saved: but for the elect's sake those days shall be shortened." (Matt. 24:22), because Jesus's return will come before humanity has the chance to annihilate itself, which became possible when we dropped the first atomic bomb.

The Jewish diaspora ended when Jesus fulfilled prophecy by helping Israel become a nation in 1948, ending thousands of years of exile and calling the Jewish people home to Jerusalem, "And when ye shall see Jerusalem compassed with armies, then know that the desolation thereof is nigh. Then let them which are in Judaea flee to the mountains; and let them which are in the midst of it depart out; and let not them that are in the countries enter thereinto. For these be the days of vengeance, that all things which are written may be fulfilled." (Lk. 21:20-22), those living before 1948 would not have believed the creation of a Jewish state was likely. But with God, all things are possible, and now Jerusalem is part of the nation of Israel, fulfilling that part of this prophecy. And Israel is surrounded by enemy armies, who have unsuccessfully attempted to destroy Israel twice, 1967 and 1973. But God protected Israel both times.

Jesus continues to inspire us to spread His Word to the uttermost part of the earth, "And this gospel of the kingdom shall be preached in all the world for a witness unto all nations; and then shall the end come." (Matt. 24:14). Today, many of God's servants are working hard to fulfill this prophecy, and it will be completed soon.

God had Daniel give us this prophecy, "But thou, O Daniel, shut up the words, and seal the book, even to the time of the end: many shall run to and fro, and knowledge shall be increased." (Dan. 12:4), so 2,500 years later we might experience their fulfillment and thus have our faith bolstered by air travel becoming commonplace and the internet's continually making knowledge more accessible.

Jesus is patiently waiting for the correct number of us to prepare ourselves for the wedding to come, "Let us be glad and rejoice, and give honour to him: for the marriage of the Lamb is come, and his wife hath made herself ready." (Rev. 19:7). And it will be a giant celebration. He already knows who among us will choose to live with Him. But, He also knows we need to go through the sanctification process, like David, Moses, and Saul did before they were fit for His kingdom. So, He patiently waits for us.

We could choose to remain trapped in our doubt, or we could allow Jesus to teach us God's wisdom, which will then lead us to the truth being hidden amongst the lies of this world, "If any of you lack wisdom, let him ask of God, that giveth to all men liberally, and upbraideth not; and it shall be given him." (Jam. 1:5). Jesus is doing exactly what He needs to do. He is calling us to come home to Him.

CHAPTER 9
Our Evil Ways

So, what are our evil ways? And how do we turn away from them?

Let us compare this life to a great war to better understand evil. The goal of God's side has always been to bring the truth to all who would be saved. Lucifer was the first to rebel, "For thou hast said in thine heart, I will ascend into heaven, I will exalt my throne above the stars of God: I will sit also upon the mount of the congregation, in the sides of the north: I will ascend above the heights of the clouds; I will be like the most High." (Isa. 14:13-14), and Lucifer began this war believing he could replace God. This is the only war that matters, and it is now being fought for our souls. God uses love, truth, and freedom as His only weapons in this war. He does not need any other weapons because He already knows how it will end. The devil uses selfishness, hatred, lies, addictions, slavery, unnecessary laws, pain, suffering, coercion, punishment, etc., as his weapons to keep us from the truth. All who have tasted the pleasures of this life know how addicting they can be, but God never tempts us, He offers us His love and eternity to enjoy it, "Blessed is the man that endureth temptation: for when he is tried, he shall receive the crown of life, which the Lord hath promised to them that love him. Let no man say when he is tempted, I am tempted of God: for God cannot be tempted with evil, neither tempteth he any man: But every man is tempted, when he is drawn away of his own lust, and enticed. Then when lust hath conceived, it bringeth forth sin: and sin, when it is finished, bringeth forth death." (Jam. 1:12-15).

The devil does not want us to compare the temporary pleasures he offers to the eternal peace and joy God is offering. So, he complicates our lives and captures our minds with music, strife, alcohol, drugs, and mind-numbing games to minimize the time we have to thoroughly investigate our choices; and keep us from recognizing our addictions. The devil wants us to think God is our enemy. Did God act like our enemy when He sent Jesus to die on that cross for us? Jesus calls to us from that cross. He wants us to choose Him and God's weapons, love, truth, and freedom. If we are not sure whose side we have been supporting, we need only look at the weapons we have used. Do we love everyone? Have we reasoned to find the truth, or have we accepted opinions without testing them? Are we allowing others the freedom to live this life as they choose, or do we want them to do what we believe they should?

Before I picked up my cross, I thought I knew what makes a person good. I thought I was better than most, and I did not need to change. However, once I accepted God's love, I began to see the truth about the weapons I was using, "For if any be a hearer of the word, and not a doer, he is like unto a man beholding his natural face in a glass: For he beholdeth himself, and goeth his way, and straightway forgetteth what manner of man he was." (Jam. 1:23-24), and my conscious mind finally recognized the guilt my subconscious had been hiding. Seeing my life reflected in my spiritual mirror for the first time was a harrowing experience. The conflicts I had been living with were now fully exposed. My faith in Jesus allows the love of God to transform me and the weapons I choose to wield, "But whoso looketh into the perfect law of liberty, and continueth therein, he being not a forgetful hearer, but a doer of the work, this man shall be blessed in his deed." (Jam. 1:25). And my relationships have improved. I know I am not perfect, I am not the man I dream of becoming, and I know I cannot complete this process myself, so, I continually surrender to His will, knowing He will finish this work upon His return, "In a moment, in the twinkling of an eye, at the last trump: for the trumpet shall sound, and the dead shall be raised incorruptible, and we shall be changed." (1 Cor. 15:52). It is a process, and I am learning to enjoy the progress.

God tells us, we are either with Him or against Him, "He that is not with me is against me; and he that gathereth not with me scattereth abroad." (Matt. 12:30), so we can understand we are making a decision, either consciously or unconsciously. If we allow our apathy to keep us from gathering with Him, we will be led away from God and participate in scattering instead. We are in the middle of a spiritual war with eternal consequences, "For we wrestle not against flesh and blood, but against principalities, against powers, against the rulers of the darkness of this world, against spiritual wickedness in high places." (Eph. 6:12). This war is defined by love and eternity. There is only one Being capable of granting us entry into eternity, and all we have to do is accept His love.

So, in this life, either we choose God's side, or we will be lost in the illusions of this shadow world, and eternally separated from His love, "Who shall be punished with everlasting destruction from the presence of the Lord, and from the glory of his power;" (2 Thess. 1:9). If we do not choose Jesus, it will not matter which other path we end up on; alcoholism or sobriety, crime or purity, atheism or another religion, anger or humility, etcetera, for they all end in death. This world is not our home. There is too much anger, hatred, and suffering.

God does not censor evil behavior nor the sacrifices required along the path to Him; He even exposes the evil done by the Bible's heroes. He describes both sides, so we can compare them and ultimately learn there is a difference between good and evil, "And be not conformed to this world: but be ye transformed by the renewing of your mind, that ye may prove what is that good, and acceptable, and perfect, will of God." (Rom. 12:2). We can learn about the World War II concentration camps, which are still being preserved as museums rather than destroyed. Those concentration camps keep the truth of that genocide before us, so we can know the kinds of damage evil does with the weapons it chooses to use. Nazi Germany killed millions of innocent people during World War II. No one should be able to convince us it was made up. Evil wants to destroy anything that could be used to expose it. Criminals kill witnesses who could testify against them, just as ISIS destroyed evidence of anything that contradicted their message. And, we have seen similar actions here in our own country. Until we learn that we are called by God to question everything, both sides of every issue, we will be led by those with the power to control the narrative before us. This attempt to stifle free speech and destroy everything that symbolizes opposition is a demonstration of evil.

Evil is trying to convince us we can know it all, that our memories are perfect, that we have learned all we need to know from history's mistakes, that we have never changed our minds on any issue, so we do not need to hear both sides of every issue. How are we supposed to reason with ideas when one side is being hidden or systematically destroyed? What are those who hide or destroy history afraid of? God does not tell us to ignore the evil messages. Instead, He asks us to test them against His message of love, to determine what is good, "Prove all things; hold fast that which is good. Abstain from all appearance of evil." (1 Thess. 5:21-22). God wants us to abstain from anything that might appear evil, but we need to compare both sides to know which one is evil. He asks us to avoid evil because people are waiting to use our actions to convict God since we are His representatives in this world. This is what they tried to do to Jesus, "And they send unto him certain of the Pharisees and of the Herodians, to catch him in his words." (Mk. 12:13). Evil is selfish, hypocritical, and not interested in the truth, only in having its own way. And evil will do anything to silence the opposition, including violently attacking us to stifle the spreading of God's Word. We cannot let the actions of a few thoughtless people, cowards hiding behind the anonymity of the mob, affect our eternal future.

Listen as God describes the behavior we can look for on His side of this war, "Either make the tree good, and his fruit good; or else make the tree corrupt, and his fruit corrupt: for the tree is known by his fruit." (Matt. 12:33), and "And now abideth faith, hope, charity, these three; but the greatest of these is charity." (1 Cor. 13:13), and "I therefore, the prisoner of the Lord, beseech you that ye walk worthy of the vocation wherewith ye are called, With all lowliness and meekness, with longsuffering, forbearing one another in love; Endeavouring to keep the unity of the Spirit in the bond of peace." (Eph. 4:1-3), and "By pureness, by knowledge, by long suffering, by kindness, by the Holy Ghost, by love unfeigned, By the word of truth, by the power of God, by the armour of righteousness on the right hand and on the left," (2 Cor. 6:6-7), and "Put on therefore, as the elect of God, holy and beloved, bowels of mercies, kindness, humbleness of mind, meekness, longsuffering;" (Col. 3:12), and "My little children, let us not love in word, neither in tongue; but in deed and in truth." (1 Jn. 3:18). Can it be any clearer? God knows us by our fruit, and we cannot blame someone else for the fruit we are producing.

Jesus promises us His peace; no matter what is going on around us, all we need to do is have faith, "I exhort therefore, that, first of all, supplications, prayers, intercessions, and giving of thanks, be made for all men; For kings, and for all that are in authority; that we may lead a quiet and peaceable life in all godliness and honesty." (1 Tim. 2:1-4). Is God saying this step will prepare our minds for what is to come? Of course, it will, because the hope Jesus brought us will be deeply rooted in our hearts, "Who his own self bare our sins in his own body on the tree, that we, being dead to sins, should live unto righteousness: by whose stripes ye were healed." (1 Pet. 2:24). This leads us to use only God's weapons of love, truth, and freedom. This leads us to peacefully accept the sacrifices we make in this war to save souls from eternal death. What sacrifice is too great to save even one soul? The military slogan, "no man left behind," is an echo of Jesus's words, urging us to save as many souls as we can, "How think ye? if a man have an hundred sheep, and one of them be gone astray, doth he not leave the ninety and nine, and goeth into the mountains, and seeketh that which is gone astray?" (Matt. 18:12). Can we imagine a marine saying, "my life is worth more, so I am going to leave that person behind?" Can we imagine anyone in love with Jesus saying that?

In war, there are victims. Jesus formed a small group of followers and directed them to spread the truth of His love to the uttermost part of the earth, "And this gospel of the kingdom shall be preached in all the world for a witness unto all nations; and then shall the end come." (Matt. 24:14). That small group grew to be one-third of the Roman Empire before Constantine became Emperor. How did this happen? There was no formal evangelistic effort beyond the sharing of His love. This was nothing short of a miracle, considering the enemy was feeding those early Christians to the lions, boiling them alive, crucifying them, and every one of their original leaders suffered horrible deaths. Despite all this adversity, their lives contrasted God's love with the selfishness of evil, and it drew people to Jesus and His way. Once we see His love in action, we are drawn to it; some respond by following Him, and some of us find it too painful because we finally understand we cannot hide our sins from God, "Whither shall I go from thy spirit? or whither shall I flee from thy presence?" (Ps. 139:7). When we refuse His salvation, our sins are left unresolved, eating away at our lives, joy, peace, and happiness. This leaves us with a problem. We have to accept His forgiveness, run from Him, or strike out at Him. Is this the reason we have seen so much hatred and violence against Christians these past 2,000 years?

True Christians are no threat to anyone because they are living under God's law of love, "Love worketh no ill to his neighbour: therefore love is the fulfilling of the law." (Rom. 13:10), and "Follow peace with all men, and holiness, without which no man shall see the Lord:" (Heb. 12:14). So, why do so many people hate Christians? Why are they willing to persecute them? Why do some want to kill those actively living God's law of love? Is it their guilt being exposed by the fruit of the Spirit? The latest published statistics show that Christians are still being killed every day for their belief. Try searching "Christians dying for their faith" to learn more about this tragedy. God told us why people would hate us, "If the world hate you, ye know that it hated me before it hated you." (Jn. 15:18) and "Casting down imaginations, and every high thing that exalteth itself against the knowledge of God, and bringing into captivity every thought to the obedience of Christ;" (2 Cor. 10:5). God's Word casts down imaginations and brings them into captivity leading to obedience and the world hates us for it.

The spiritual war between God and Satan has victims, some of us who choose God's side will be injured, and some will become martyrs, even in our country. The 26 wounded and the 20 killed, at Sutherland Springs Church in Texas, on November 5, 2017, and the 9 killed at Emanuel African Methodist Episcopal Church in Charleston, South Carolina, on June 16, 2015, are examples. The family members of those 9 victims killed at the Emanuel Church stood up during the trial and told Dylann Roof that they forgave him for murdering their family members. This is the best possible Christian response, and it serves to emphasize the difference between true Christians and those who hate us. It demonstrates the life God calls us to live. He wants us to be lights shining in a dark world. We turn from our evil ways when we choose to love everyone, always tell the truth, and allow others to have the same freedom to decide for themselves. Who has ever been hurt by Christians acting this way? But how do we do this?

We must refuse to allow Satan to shackle us with his addictions, "Stand fast therefore in the liberty wherewith Christ hath made us free, and be not entangled again with the yoke of bondage." (Gal. 5:1). Unlike the person who tries cocaine to experience the high, ultimately suffering from the addiction, we choose to refuse Satan's offer.

We must choose to use our freedom for good, not allowing maliciousness to creep into our lives, "As free, and not using your liberty for a cloke of maliciousness, but as the servants of God." (1 Pet. 2:16). We must choose to live the fruits of the Spirit, which God freely offers to all, "But now being made free from sin, and become servants to God, ye have your fruit unto holiness, and the end everlasting life." (Rom. 6:22). We do not allow corruption or vanity to enter our lives, "This I say therefore, and testify in the Lord, that ye henceforth walk not as other Gentiles walk, in the vanity of their mind," (Eph. 4:17)

We must work to free the oppressed, "Is not this the fast that I have chosen? to loose the bands of wickedness, to undo the heavy burdens, and to let the oppressed go free, and that ye break every yoke? Is it not to deal thy bread to the hungry, and that thou bring the poor that are cast out to thy house? when thou seest the naked, that thou cover him; and that thou hide not thyself from thine own flesh?" (Isa. 58:6-7). We do not use the gospel to burden others, "Now therefore why tempt ye God, to put a yoke upon the neck of the disciples, which neither our fathers nor we were able to bear?" (Acts 15:10).

We do not judge others, "Conscience, I say, not thine own, but of the other: for why is my liberty judged of another man's conscience?" (1 Cor. 10:29).

We are humble and live peacefully with all people, "Render therefore to all their dues: tribute to whom tribute is due; custom to whom custom; fear to whom fear; honour to whom honour. Owe no man any thing, but to love one another: for he that loveth another hath fulfilled the law." (Rom. 13:7-8). We willingly sacrifice our freedoms when they would cause our brothers to stumble, "Wherefore, if meat make my brother to offend, I will eat no flesh while the world standeth, lest I make my brother to offend." (1 Cor. 8:13). This means we need to think about how our actions affect others.

Loving our neighbors means we do not force our choices onto them, and we allow them the freedom to love God or not without judging them. At first, this is a difficult position to understand. Our world keeps telling us we need to judge everything and everyone, by our political opinions. This world wants us to take a position, to be divided into groups, eventually losing our ability to have our own opinions. We no longer need to think; our group will tell us what to believe. Watching our congress vote on issues validates this description. Do all Republicans and all Democrats need to vote in blocks on every issue? Why do we even need elected officials if they will not think for themselves?

Taking a very controversial topic and discussing it from God's point of view might help our reasoning. Most people would readily agree that God would be against abortion since He never aborts us when we live in disobedience to His way. Instead, He loves us and supports us, always offering us an eternal life of joy. God only asks us to love as He does, so we will aid in the gathering rather than causing others pain and separating them from God. Rather than pointing our self-righteous fingers, He wants us to gather in support of a pregnant woman feeling overwhelmed. He wants us to financially support them if they need it during their pregnancy. He wants us to help that mother and baby if she decides to keep the baby. He wants us to offer to find a home for the baby if the mother is unwilling to care for it. Most importantly, He wants us to show His unconditional love for them, both mother and baby. This is how we abide in His love and fight for His side in this war against evil.

And, He calls us to use only God's weapons of love, truth, and freedom in the war we face daily, "From whence come wars and fightings among you? come they not hence, even of your lusts that war in your members?" (Jam. 4:1). Can we not see our lack of love for others is causing the fighting in our world? God tells us we are all created in His image, so what is there to fight about?

Just as we see the results of defying the natural laws He created, like gravity, we will ultimately see the consequences of disobeying God's law of love, "For my thoughts are not your thoughts, neither are your ways my ways, saith the Lord. For as the heavens are higher than the earth, so are my ways higher than your ways, and my thoughts than your thoughts." (Isa. 55:8-9). Some of us will do anything to quiet our conscience, including replacing the truth of God with fables created by man, or the devil, "Then I sent unto him, saying, There are no such things done as thou sayest, but thou feignest them out of thine own heart." (Neh. 6:8), and "Beware of false prophets, which come to you in sheep's clothing, but inwardly they are ravening wolves." (Matt. 7:15), and "Howbeit in vain do they worship me, teaching for doctrines the commandments of men." (Mk. 7:7), and "If any man teach otherwise, and consent not to wholesome words, even the words of our Lord Jesus Christ, and to the doctrine which is according to godliness; He is proud, knowing nothing, but doting about questions and strifes of words, whereof cometh envy, strife, railings, evil surmisings," (1 Tim. 6:3-4), and "Be sober, be vigilant; because your adversary the devil, as a roaring lion, walketh about, seeking whom he may devour:" (1 Pet. 5:8), but there are no satisfying answers for this life without God. No matter how hard we fight, no matter what else we cling to, no matter what other kind of god we create, life is never as good, and eternity will never be attainable without God.

In short, we choose to build our lives upon His overwhelming, never-ending, uninhibited love, rather than the selfish pleasures of this world, by daily reading and reasoning with His Word, which is why He told us about our daily bread, "Give us this day our daily bread." (Matt. 6:11). It will make all the difference when He returns. And, He will return, "In my Father's house are many mansions: if it were not so, I would have told you. I go to prepare a place for you. And if I go and prepare a place for you, I will come again, and receive you unto myself; that where I am, there ye may be also." (Jn. 14:2), for He cannot lie, "In hope of eternal life, which God, that cannot lie, promised before the world began;" (Tit. 1:2).

CHAPTER 10
Our Journey to Him

This book describes the journey God has created for us and why this journey is necessary. This journey leads some onto the path of His love, taking our disbelief to belief, then faith, and finally works. For faith is required for salvation and works are the fruits, which are produced by our faith, "For by grace are ye saved through faith; and that not of yourselves: it is the gift of God: Not of works, lest any man should boast … (For the fruit of the Spirit is in all goodness and righteousness and truth;)" (Eph. 2:8-9, 5:9). Make no mistake; God says we are not saved by works. However, we are not saved without works, "For as the body without the spirit is dead, so faith without works is dead also." (Jam. 2:20), and "If any man among you seem to be religious, and bridleth not his tongue, but deceiveth his own heart, this man's religion is vain. Pure religion and undefiled before God and the Father is this, To visit the fatherless and widows in their affliction, and to keep himself unspotted from the world." (Jam. 1:26-27). This is why He told us faith without works is dead, "But wilt thou know, O vain man, that faith without works is dead?" (Jam. 2:26). When we have faith only, our vanity causes us to misunderstand His Word, which leads us to create denominations since we think we know God better than others. This is why He calls us to have the faith of a little child, which requires us to humble ourselves, "And said, Verily I say unto you, Except ye be converted, and become as little children, ye shall not enter into the kingdom of heaven." (Matt. 18:3), because little children know they are needy, and so do the humble. Only the humble can be reasonable enough to come together and reason with God's Word rather than arguing their understanding is better than everyone else's.

God is telling us true faith requires action because we have a part to play in the creation of His kingdom, "But ye shall receive power, after that the Holy Ghost is come upon you: and ye shall be witnesses unto me both in Jerusalem, and in all Judaea, and in Samaria, and unto the uttermost part of the earth." (Acts 1:8). God is not calling us to be an audience; He wants a family willing to help Him build His kingdom, as Noe and Moses did. His Word comes to life when we understand this, and it changes us from the inside out, from apathetic angels to Jesus's friends. Faith in action is not only the big things but also the little things we do to shine His light on heaven's door. He created us to solve problems, not complain about them. We are God's cure being dispensed in this infected world. A world filled with the lusts of the eyes, the lusts of the flesh and the pride of life, "For all that is in the world, the lust of the flesh, and the lust of the eyes, and the pride of life, is not of the Father, but is of the world." (1 Jn. 2:16). God's cure is the example seen when His saints are joyfully walking through sanctification to eternity.

God is telling us life is more than a mental exercise, "Wherefore the Lord said, Forasmuch as this people draw near me with their mouth, and with their lips do honour me, but have removed their heart far from me, and their fear toward me is taught by the precept of men:" (Isa. 29:13), and "But be ye doers of the word, and not hearers only, deceiving your own selves … Yea, a man may say, Thou hast faith, and I have works: shew me thy faith without thy works, and I will shew thee my faith by my works … For as the body without the spirit is dead, so faith without works is dead also." (Jam. 1:22, 2:18, 26). Going to church once a week and living the rest of our lives reconciled to this world will not lead to our transformation, our sanctification, "I beseech you therefore, brethren, by the mercies of God, that ye present your bodies a living sacrifice, holy, acceptable unto God, which is your reasonable service. And be not conformed to this world: but be ye transformed by the renewing of your mind, that ye may prove what is that good, and acceptable, and perfect, will of God." (Rom. 12:1-2).

The closer we come to completing our part in God's plan, the more He gives us to do, "His lord said unto him, Well done, good and faithful servant; thou hast been faithful over a few things, I will make thee ruler over many things: enter thou into the joy of thy lord." (Matt. 25:23), and "Take therefore the talent from him, and give it unto him which hath ten talents." (Matt. 25:28), and "For unto every one that hath shall be given, and he shall have abundance: but from him that hath not shall be taken away even that which he hath." (Matt. 25:29).

Some will understand the journey, while others of us will twist and distort it for our own purposes, lying even to ourselves. Sometimes these distortions are to ease the pain caused by the conflicts lived with daily, which our separation from God created, "That at that time ye were without Christ, being aliens from the commonwealth of Israel, and strangers from the covenants of promise, having no hope, and without God in the world." (Eph 2:12). Sometimes they are to gain some temporary advantage or pleasure, "The prophets prophesy falsely, and the priests bear rule by their means; and my people love to have it so: and what will ye do in the end thereof?" (Jer. 5:31). But our desires and/or distortions will not change the truth of the journey, nor the ultimate destinations, "My covenant will I not break, nor alter the thing that is gone out of my lips." (Ps. 89:34), and "Therefore as the fire devoureth the stubble, and the flame consumeth the chaff, so their root shall be as rottenness, and their blossom shall go up as dust: because they have cast away the law of the Lord of hosts, and despised the word of the Holy One of Israel." (Isa. 5:24).

Jesus prayed for all of us to be one in Him, as He is one in the Father, "Neither pray I for these alone, but for them also which shall believe on me through their word; That they all may be one; as thou, Father, art in me, and I in thee, that they also may be one in us: that the world may believe that thou hast sent me. And the glory which thou gavest me I have given them; that they may be one, even as we are one:" (Jn. 17:20-22). Jesus told us when we see Him, we see the Father, for He is one with the Father, "Jesus saith unto him, Have I been so long time with you, and yet hast thou not known me, Philip? he that hath seen me hath seen the Father; and how sayest thou then, Show us the Father?" (Jn. 14:9). God says there is only one eternal family, and His Word is being preached so all may have the opportunity to find their way to Him and His family. His offer goes out to every one of us. The key is not that we are all different in some ways because He has given each of us a unique DNA; the key is that we are all the same in many more ways, as we are all made in His image, "So God created man in his own image, in the image of God created he him; male and female created he them." (Gen. 1:27).

The devil uses divisions to keep us from coming together to reason on the important issues, which would lead us to love and care for one another, "If I then, your Lord and Master, have washed your feet; ye also ought to wash one another's feet." (Jn. 13:14), and "And if one prevail against him, two shall withstand him; and a threefold cord is not quickly broken." (Eccl. 4:12). Can we imagine what it would be like for all of us to peacefully come together to reason, bringing our opinions and our willingness to consider other opinions?

God is not creating all the artificial divisions that exist in our lives. He is also not creating the many churches we see in our society. God has only one church, His church. He is asking us to lay down our differences. We can lay them at the foot of the cross, at the foot of His Word. He wants us to learn that He is love, "And we have known and believed the love that God hath to us. God is love; and he that dwelleth in love dwelleth in God, and God in him." (1 Jn. 4:16), and that we should love the way He loves, unconditionally, "Beloved, if God so loved us, we ought also to love one another." (1 Jn. 4:11). His unconditional love for us is the reason He gave us free will. He asks each of us to choose to be part of His family. This is another layer of the concept of being one, our being in Jesus, and Him in us, abiding in Him, "If ye abide in me, and my words abide in you, ye shall ask what ye will, and it shall be done unto you." (Jn. 15:7).

He wants us to learn to love, in this life, to prepare us for eternity with Him as part of His family, "But love ye your enemies, and do good, and lend, hoping for nothing again; and your reward shall be great, and ye shall be the children of the Highest: for he is kind unto the unthankful and to the evil." (Lk 6:35). Separating ourselves means we want to live our own way or one of the many ways the devil has established to lead us away from God instead of following His way and the peace and joy that will undoubtedly follow. We can choose to be part of His family; however, when we refuse, He will allow us to go our own way, which leads to death, not eternity, "There is a way which seemeth right unto a man, but the end thereof are the ways of death." (Prov. 14:12). But, when we follow Jesus, "But the wisdom that is from above is first pure, then peaceable, gentle, and easy to be intreated, full of mercy and good fruits, without partiality, and without hypocrisy." (Jam. 3:17), we use good to overcome evil, "Be not overcome of evil, but overcome evil with good." (Rom. 12:21).

The devil's temptations always lead us to divisions, distress, and ultimately death. When we follow that path away from God, we will never find true love, peace, and joy; no matter how much money, power, fame, or pretend holiness we have, "He that loveth silver shall not be satisfied with silver; nor he that loveth abundance with increase: this is also vanity." (Eccl. 5:10). The devil's fleshy temptations drive us away from God, but God sends His Spirit to draw us to Him, "For they that are after the flesh do mind the things of the flesh; but they that are after the Spirit the things of the Spirit." (Rom. 8:5). When we choose to follow the Spirit, the things of the flesh begin to dim, "For to be carnally minded is death; but to be spiritually minded is life and peace. Because the carnal mind is enmity against God:

for it is not subject to the law of God, neither indeed can be." (Rom. 8:6-7), and eventually, we desire God's law of love rather than the temptations of this world.

Something inside is telling us there is more to this life than eating, sleeping, having sex, doing drugs, and getting ahead of the next person in line, for God not only wrote His story, He placed it in every heart, "But this shall be the covenant that I will make with the house of Israel; After those days, saith the Lord, I will put my law in their inward parts, and write it in their hearts; and will be their God, and they shall be my people." (Jer. 31:33), and "Forasmuch as ye are manifestly declared to be the epistle of Christ ministered by us, written not with ink, but with the Spirit of the living God; not in tables of stone, but in fleshy tables of the heart." (2 Cor. 3:3).

God's message is clear, "When Jesus therefore saw his mother, and the disciple standing by, whom he loved, he saith unto his mother, Woman, behold thy son! Then saith he to the disciple, Behold thy mother! And from that hour that disciple took her unto his own home." (Jn. 19:26-27). In telling John to care for His mother, Jesus was also telling us to care for each other. We are to take care of others, demonstrating God's love for them, and when they choose to come to Jesus, they will recognize their sins and begin the process of removing their barnacles.

God promises to take care of us, "Fear thou not; for I am with thee: be not dismayed; for I am thy God: I will strengthen thee; yea, I will help thee; yea, I will uphold thee with the right hand of my righteousness." (Isa. 41:10), and this assurance gives us the courage to follow Him. He wants everyone to feel His love, and each of us has the opportunity to receive salvation by accepting His love, "For God, who commanded the light to shine out of darkness, hath shined in our hearts, to give the light of the knowledge of the glory of God in the face of Jesus Christ." (2 Cor. 4:6).

Some will choose not to hear that still small voice that is calling us home, and we will not follow Him, "She obeyed not the voice; she received not correction; she trusted not in the Lord; she drew not near to her God." (Zeph. 3:2). The still small voice led Moses, Joseph, Daniel, John, Peter Waldo, and so many others to do God's work, and it will teach anyone willing to come close enough to God to hear it. God could shout, however, then we would be afraid of Him and would start creating harsher versions of Him, as the Israelites did, "And they said unto Moses, Speak thou with us, and we will hear: but let not God speak with us, lest we die." (Ex. 20:19). So, He whispers to us with a still small voice, as we do to our babies when they are crying, because He loves us even when we are wallowing in our sins, "But God, who is rich in mercy, for his great love wherewith he loved us, Even when we were dead in sins, hath quickened us together with Christ, (by grace ye are saved;)" (Eph. 2:4-5), and "And after the earthquake a fire; but the Lord was not in the fire: and after the fire a still small voice." (1 Kgs. 19:12).

God has offered us a way that leads to His peace and joy, "The LORD will give strength unto his people; the LORD will bless his people with peace." (Ps. 29:11). I recently heard a pastor explaining how accepting the truth of God's Word helps us live a more peaceful and joyful life. He told a story of watching the replay of a football game he already knew his team had won. However, late in the replay, they turned the ball over, and it seemed all was lost. Instead of being upset, he felt excited because he knew he was about to witness something special. His team was going to pull off a miracle win. God has already told us about the new earth He is creating. We just need to believe He will pull off all of the miracles required to produce the win He has prophesied, "And I saw a new heaven and a new earth: for the first heaven and the first earth were passed away; and there was no more sea. And I John saw the holy city, new Jerusalem, coming down from God out of heaven, prepared as a bride adorned for her husband. And I heard a great voice out of heaven saying, Behold, the tabernacle of God is with men, and he will dwell with them, and they shall be his people, and God himself shall be with them, and be their God." (Rev. 21:1-3), and it is our faith that allows us to see past the turnovers of this life. This leads us to the eternity He is creating. Nothing can change the expected end He has planned, so we can relax and enjoy the journey.

We are to show His love to others by abiding in His love, so they will be able to witness our example, "Let your light so shine before men, that they may see your good works, and glorify your Father which is in heaven." (Matt. 5:16), which draws them to Him, as we become His lights shining in this world and reducing the number of dark places for evil to hide. God's love is pure and self-sacrificing, "Herein is love, not that we loved God, but that he loved us, and sent his Son to be the propitiation for our sins." (1 Jn. 4:10). We live in a world of self-promotion, a "look at me" world, an "I know better" world, "This know also, that in the last days perilous times shall come. For men shall be lovers of their own selves, covetous, boasters, proud, blasphemers, disobedient to parents, unthankful, unholy, Without natural affection, trucebreakers, false accusers, incontinent, fierce, despisers of those that are good, Traitors, heady, highminded, lovers of pleasures more than lovers of God;" (2 Tim. 3:1-4). The contrast could not be more dramatic. Loving others means we joyfully serve them, "For, brethren, ye have been called unto liberty; only use not liberty for an occasion to the flesh, but by love serve one another." (Gal. 5:13), expecting nothing in return. And we must allow others to serve us, "Peter saith unto him, Thou shalt never wash my feet. Jesus answered him, If I wash thee not, thou hast no part with me. Simon Peter saith unto him, Lord, not my feet only, but also my hands and my head." (Jn. 13:8-9). We cannot deprive others of the joy of serving.

God is not asking us to figure it out. He is asking us to trust Him to have already done that, "So shall my word be that goeth forth out of my mouth: it shall not return unto me void, but it shall accomplish that which I please, and it shall prosper in the thing whereto I sent it." (Isa. 55:11). We just need to accept His love and give it away to everyone we meet, to the uttermost part of the earth. He created us to do this work, and we put a smile upon His face when we do.

The eternity God calls us to will be filled with peace and joy. No one there will be causing pain or tears, "And God shall wipe away all tears from their eyes; and there shall be no more death, neither sorrow, nor crying, neither shall there be any more pain: for the former things are passed away." (Rev. 21:4). We just need to understand He is not asking us to wait for heaven to live that life. Instead, He asks us to live His law of love in this life. He asks us to live in that convergent space where heaven and earth kiss, shining our light and leading others to Him and eternity. This means we choose to live a life that will not cause others pain. A life that demonstrates we genuinely want to live an eternal life as part of His family.

Jesus has called us His friends, "Henceforth I call you not servants; for the servant knoweth not what his lord doeth: but I have called you friends; for all things that I have heard of my Father I have made known unto you." (Jn. 15:15). Are we living as though we believe we are His friends? If we live His law of love, always telling the truth and allowing others the same freedom, we will be Jesus's friends for eternity.

ABOUT THE AUTHOR

Bill Cohen has read and reasoned with the Bible for over 30 years. This book is a labor of love assigned by God and now finally completed. When God calls, His friends answer.

Printed in the United States
by Baker & Taylor Publisher Services